Friendship Quilts...
THE HAWAIIAN WAY

Designs for Quilting
and Counted Cross Stitch

Elizabeth Root

XS charts & stitching by Al Hannen
Photography by Paul Kodama
Pre-press by Kym Miller

Softcover
ISBN 1-885804-41-5

Printed in China
FIRST EDITION
10 9 8 7 6 5 4 3 2 1

ERDHI
Elizabeth Root Designs Hawaii, Inc.
Post Office Box 1167
Kailua, HI 96734
email: info@quiltshawaii.com
www.QuiltsHawaii.com

"Plant the seeds of friendship,
then watch the blessings grow!"

Friendship or signature quilts are many times made from one or more of the simpler patchwork block patterns. They are easy and quick to make, using same colors or many colors. They are usually embroidered with the maker's name and joined with other blocks made by a group of friends into a quilt for one special person - celebrating a special occasion in their life.

Album quilts are most times appliquéd blocks, usually made by one person. In the case of a gift quilt, they can be made by several people using a selected color palette. Sometimes a name, sentiment or event is embroidered on the individual blocks.

Friendship Quilts...the Hawaiian Way combines these traditional methods to create Hawaiian-style quilt blocks that you and your friends can use to design your own friendship quilt masterpieces.

Many of the patterns in this book are designed for the appliqué to hug the edges of the block, leaving the centers open for the name of the maker or special sentiments to be embroidered; others can be embroidered around the edges.

What a wonderful way for a group of friends to celebrate the events in each other's lives – births, marriages, or someone, sadly, moving away. These designs can be made as a single block, friend to friend, or put into a wall or bed quilt made by many friends. While each may take only a short time to make, collectively, they will bring a lifetime of memories and comfort for a special friend.

Enjoy! ~ Elizabeth

My thanks and appreciation to the wonderful women in the Philippines who offer their beautiful appliqué and quilting skills in the making of the sample quilts in this book.

Continued...

"Plant the seeds of friendship, then watch the blessings grow!"
Let Friendship Bloom

The
Friendship

Quilt
Gallery

Patterns start on page 24

"Friendship is born at the moment when one person says to another,
'What? You too? I thought I was the only one.'" ~ Unknown

"A friend is the one who sat next to you in preschool and let you have the pretty pink crayon, when only the ugly gray one was left." ~ Unknown

Patterns start on page 40

"Nothing makes the earth so spacious as to have friends at a distance."
~ Henry David Thoreau

*"Our time in friendship has not been wasted
for memories have been made."* ~ Unknown

"A circle is round it has no end, that's how long I want to be your friend!"
~ Unknown

"Don't walk in front of me, I may not follow. Don't walk behind me,
I may not lead. Walk beside me and be my friend." ~ Albert Camus

Patterns start on page 72

"Good friends are hard to find, harder to leave, and impossible to forget."
~Unknown

"In the sweetness of friendship let there be laughter,
and sharing of pleasures." ~ Kahil Gibran

Patterns start on page 74

"Walking with a friend in the dark is better than
walking alone in the light." ~ Helen Keller

"Remember me with smiles and laughs, as that's how I'll remember you."
~Unknown

"Once in an age, God sends some of us a friend who loves us...
not the person we are, but the angel we might be." ~ Harriet Beecher Stowe

Patterns start on page 86

"Whatever you do for your friend do not try to teach her cat to sing.
It only wastes your time and annoys the cat." ~ Unknown

"You'll always be my best friend, you know too much."
~ Unknown

The Cross Stitch Gallery

Bird of Paradise
114   Chart
115   Stitched Design

Passion Flower
120   Chart
121   Stitched Design

Blue Jade
116   Chart
117   Stitched Design

Pink Ginger
122   Chart
123   Stitched Design

Orchid
118   Chart
119   Stitched Design

Plumeria
124   Chart
125   Stitched Design

Pua Kenikeni

126   Chart
127   Stitched Design

Tahitian Gardenia

132   Chart
133   Stitched Design

Spiderlily

128   Chart
129   Stitched Design

Torch Ginger

134   Chart
135   Stitched Design

Star Flower

130   Chart
131   Stitched Design

Vinca

136   Chart
137   Stitched Design

Friendship quilts are intriguing. They hold so many mysteries. Who were these women who pieced together their scraps of fabric to make a personalized quilt block to be joined together, with others, for a shared friend? Did the fabrics they choose reflect their personalities? What was the occasion? Who were they? What were their lives like? So many stories, so many questions unanswered.

There is probably nothing more personal and nothing more special than a friendship quilt. To have so many spend their time thinking of you as they piece or appliqué their quilt block – selecting and laboriously embroidering their name, and perhaps a saying, so that in years to come you will fondly remember them and the friendship you shared with each.

The majority of appliqué patterns in this book are 14" square and all can be intermixed, project to project. All can be enlarged nicely to a 30" center square for a 36" or 48" wall hanging. We've done that for the Spiderlily and Anthurium wall hanging designs.

We have included fabric allowances for individual quilt blocks and borders. Depending on how you decide to use these patterns you can, then, more easily determine the total amount of each color of fabric required.

The patterns can be used in many ways in a variety of projects. The borders have been designed in sections so you can easily alter their length. Colors can be altered to suit the intended decor. The design components are provided – let your imagination inspire and guide you through your first Hawaiian-style, friendship quilt, masterpiece.

The
Quilt
Designs
& Patterns

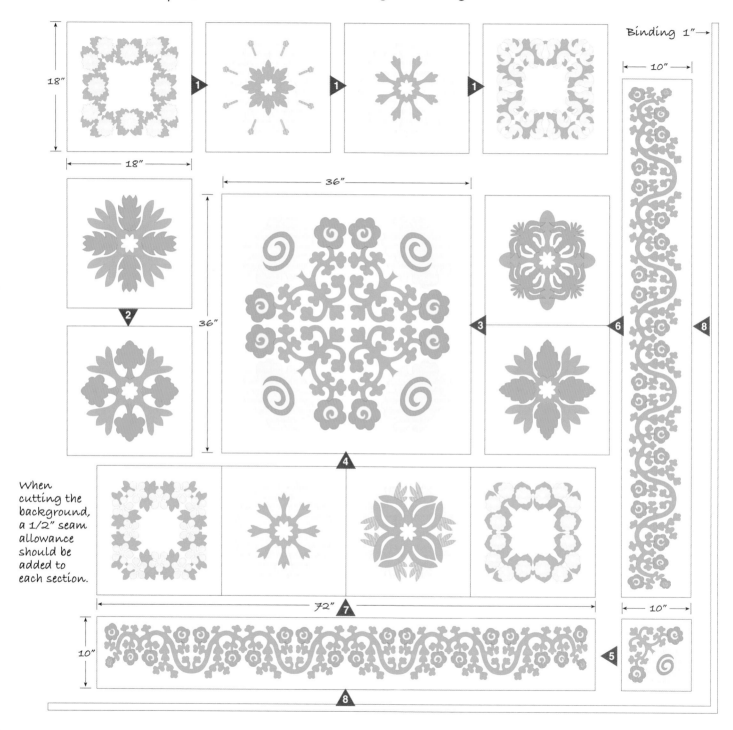

18"

18"

Binding 1"→

10"

36"

36"

When cutting the background, a 1/2" seam allowance should be added to each section.

72"

10"

10"

QUILT BLOCK PATTERNS (left to right):
ROW 1: Passion Flower, 32; Hibiscus, 30; Allamanda, 26, Blue Jade, 28;
ROW 2: Heliconia, 29; Spiderlily, 35; ROW 3: Torch Ginger, 36; Pink Ginger, 33;
ROW 4: Vinca, 37; Pua Kenikeni, 34; Bird of Paradise, 27; Morning Glory, 31;
BORDER CORNER DESIGN, 90; CENTER DESIGN, 38;
BORDER VINE DESIGN: end pattern, 91; four center sections, 92-93

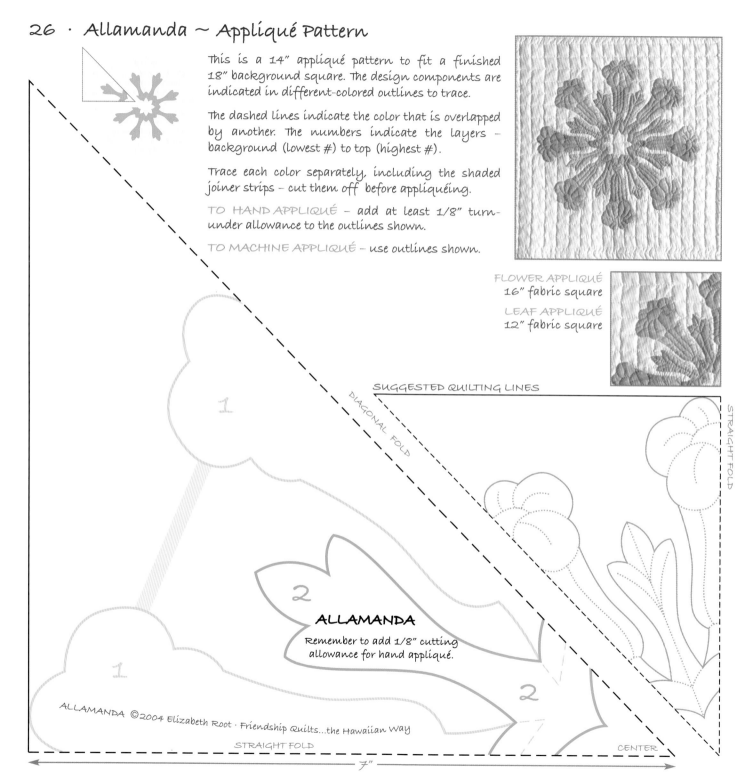

This is a 14" appliqué pattern to fit a finished 18" background square. The design components are indicated in different-colored outlines to trace.

The dashed lines indicate the color that is overlapped by another. The numbers indicate the layers – background (lowest #) to top (highest #).

Trace each color separately, including the shaded joiner strips – cut them off before appliquéing.

TO HAND APPLIQUÉ – add at least 1/8" turn-under allowance to the outlines shown.

TO MACHINE APPLIQUÉ – use outlines shown.

FLOWER APPLIQUÉ
16" fabric square

LEAF APPLIQUÉ
12" fabric square

SUGGESTED QUILTING LINES

DIAGONAL FOLD

STRAIGHT FOLD

1

2

ALLAMANDA

Remember to add 1/8" cutting allowance for hand appliqué.

1

2

2

ALLAMANDA ©2004 Elizabeth Root · Friendship Quilts...the Hawaiian Way

STRAIGHT FOLD

CENTER

7"

This is a 14" appliqué pattern to fit a finished 18" background square. The design components are indicated in different-colored outlines to trace.

The dashed lines indicate the color that is overlapped by another. The numbers indicate the layers – background (lowest #) to top (highest #).

Trace each color separately, including the shaded joiner strips – cut them off before appliquéing.

TO HAND APPLIQUÉ – add at least 1/8" turn-under allowance to the outlines shown.

TO MACHINE APPLIQUÉ – use outlines shown.

FLOWER APPLIQUÉ
16" fabric square if one color petals;
for two color petals, cut each color from eight
2-1/2" x 3-1/2" pieces of fabric.

LEAF APPLIQUÉ
12" fabric square

SUGGESTED QUILTING LINES

STRAIGHT FOLD

STRAIGHT FOLD

DIAGONAL FOLD

BIRD OF PARADISE

Remember to add 1/8" cutting allowance for hand appliqué.

1

3

2

3

Friendship Quilts...the Hawaiian way

CENTER

BIRD OF PARADISE ©2004 Elizabeth Root

STRAIGHT FOLD

7"

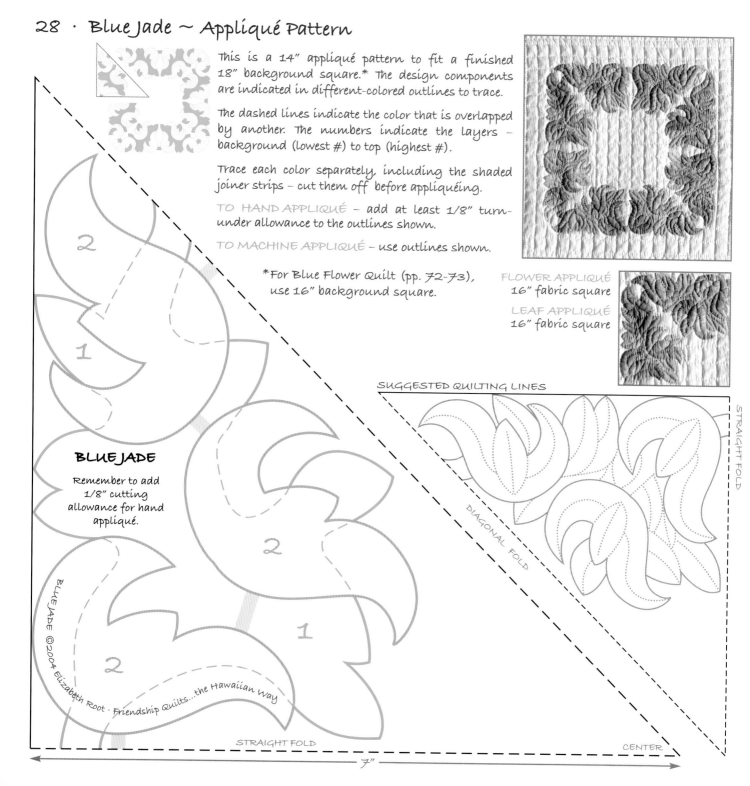

This is a 14" appliqué pattern to fit a finished 18" background square.* The design components are indicated in different-colored outlines to trace.

The dashed lines indicate the color that is overlapped by another. The numbers indicate the layers – background (lowest #) to top (highest #).

Trace each color separately, including the shaded joiner strips – cut them off before appliquéing.

TO HAND APPLIQUÉ – add at least 1/8" turn-under allowance to the outlines shown.

TO MACHINE APPLIQUÉ – use outlines shown.

*For Blue Flower Quilt (pp. 72-73), use 16" background square.

FLOWER APPLIQUÉ
16" fabric square

LEAF APPLIQUÉ
16" fabric square

BLUE JADE

Remember to add 1/8" cutting allowance for hand appliqué.

BLUE JADE ©2004 Elizabeth Root · Friendship Quilts...the Hawaiian Way

2

1

2

2

1

SUGGESTED QUILTING LINES

STRAIGHT FOLD

DIAGONAL FOLD

STRAIGHT FOLD

CENTER

7"

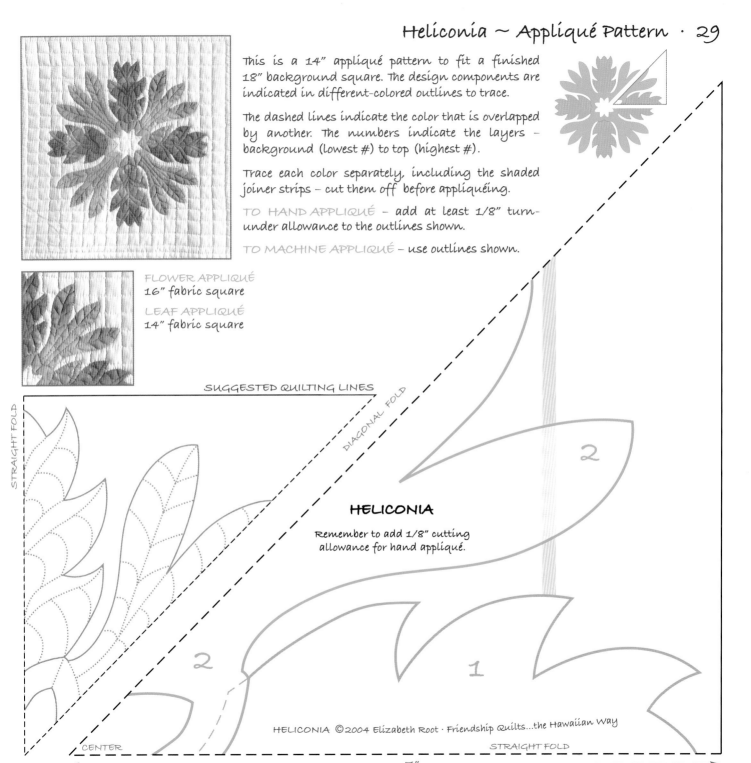

This is a 14" appliqué pattern to fit a finished 18" background square. The design components are indicated in different-colored outlines to trace.

The dashed lines indicate the color that is overlapped by another. The numbers indicate the layers – background (lowest #) to top (highest #).

Trace each color separately, including the shaded joiner strips – cut them off before appliquéing.

TO HAND APPLIQUÉ – add at least 1/8" turn-under allowance to the outlines shown.

TO MACHINE APPLIQUÉ – use outlines shown.

FLOWER APPLIQUÉ
16" fabric square

LEAF APPLIQUÉ
14" fabric square

SUGGESTED QUILTING LINES

STRAIGHT FOLD

DIAGONAL FOLD

HELICONIA

Remember to add 1/8" cutting allowance for hand appliqué.

2

2

1

CENTER

STRAIGHT FOLD

HELICONIA ©2004 Elizabeth Root · Friendship Quilts...the Hawaiian Way

7"

This is a 14" appliqué pattern to fit a finished 18" background square. The design components are indicated in different-colored outlines to trace.

The dashed lines indicate the color that is overlapped by another. The numbers indicate the layers – background (lowest #) to top (highest #).

Trace each color separately, including the shaded joiner strips – cut them off before appliquéing.

TO HAND APPLIQUÉ – add at least 1/8" turn-under allowance to the outlines shown.

TO MACHINE APPLIQUÉ – use outlines shown.

FLOWER APPLIQUÉ
16" fabric square

LEAF APPLIQUÉ
10" fabric square

STAMEN APPLIQUÉ
Cut out stamens from eight 5" x 5" fabric squares

SUGGESTED QUILTING LINES

DIAGONAL FOLD

STRAIGHT FOLD

HIBISCUS

Remember to add 1/8" cutting allowance for hand appliqué.

2

1

3

HIBISCUS ©2004 Elizabeth Root · Friendship Quilts... the Hawaiian way

STRAIGHT FOLD

CENTER

7"

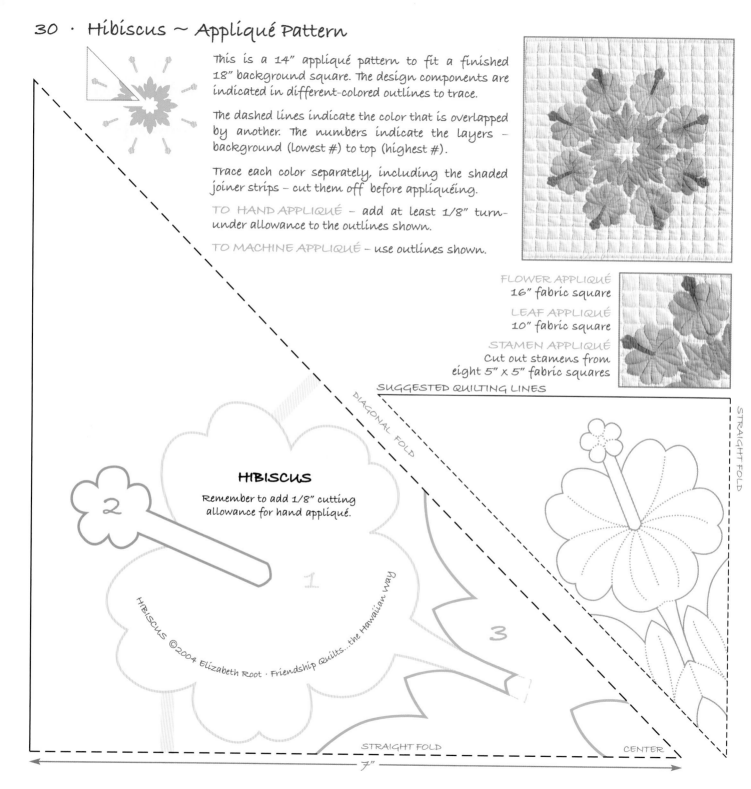

This is a 14" appliqué pattern to fit a finished 18" background square.* The design components are indicated in different-colored outlines to trace.

The dashed lines indicate the color that is overlapped by another. The numbers indicate the layers – background (lowest #) to top (highest #).

Trace each color separately, including the shaded joiner strips – cut them off before appliquéing.

TO HAND APPLIQUÉ – add at least 1/8" turn-under allowance to the outlines shown.

TO MACHINE APPLIQUÉ – use outlines shown.

FLOWER APPLIQUÉ
16" fabric square

LEAF APPLIQUÉ
16" fabric square

*For Blue Flower Quilt (pp. 72-73), use 16" background square.

SUGGESTED QUILTING LINES

STRAIGHT FOLD

DIAGONAL FOLD

MORNING GLORY

Remember to add 1/8" cutting allowance for hand appliqué.

1

2

2

1

MORNING GLORY ©2004 Elizabeth Root · Friendship Quilts... the Hawaiian way

CENTER

STRAIGHT FOLD

7"

This is a 14" appliqué pattern to fit a finished 18" background square. The design components are indicated in different-colored outlines to trace.

The dashed lines indicate the color that is overlapped by another. The numbers indicate the layers – background (lowest #) to top (highest #).

Trace each color separately, including the shaded joiner strips – cut them off before appliquéing.

TO HAND APPLIQUÉ – add at least 1/8" turn-under allowance to the outlines shown.

TO MACHINE APPLIQUÉ – use outlines shown.

*For Blue Flower Quilt (pp. 72-73), use 16" background square.

FLOWER APPLIQUÉ
16" fabric square

LEAF APPLIQUÉ
16" fabric square

SUGGESTED QUILTING LINES

DIAGONAL FOLD

STRAIGHT FOLD

1

2

PASSION FLOWER

Remember to add 1/8" cutting allowance for hand appliqué.

1

1

PASSION FLOWER ©2004 Elizabeth Root · Friendship Quilts...the Hawaiian Way

2

STRAIGHT FOLD

CENTER

7"

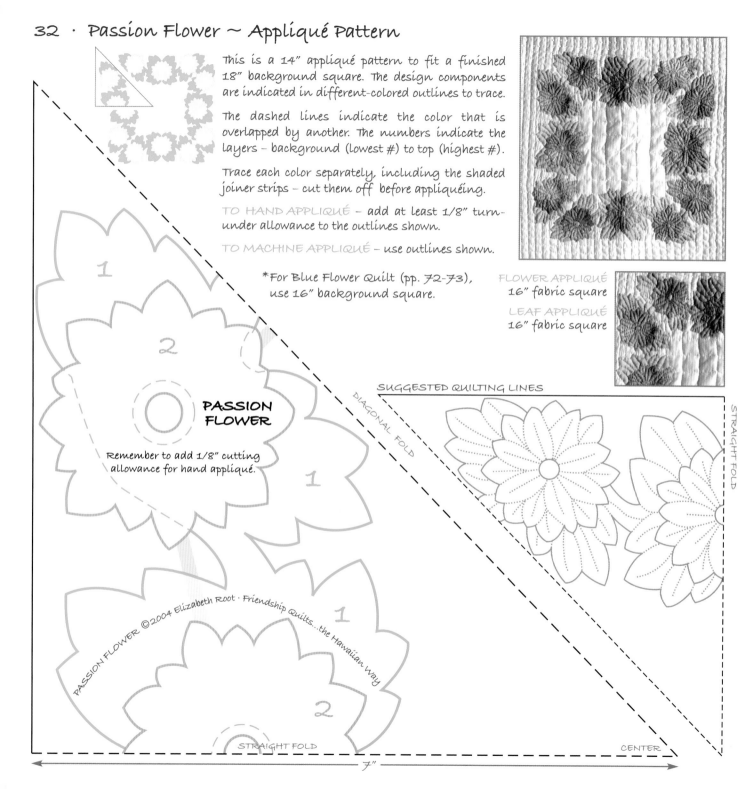

This is a 14" appliqué pattern to fit a finished 18" background square. The design components are indicated in different-colored outlines to trace.

The dashed lines indicate the color that is overlapped by another. The numbers indicate the layers – background (lowest #) to top (highest #).

Trace each color separately, including the shaded joiner strips – cut them off before appliquéing.

TO HAND APPLIQUÉ – add at least 1/8" turn-under allowance to the outlines shown.

TO MACHINE APPLIQUÉ – use outlines shown.

FLOWER APPLIQUÉ
16" fabric square

LEAF APPLIQUÉ
14" fabric square

SUGGESTED QUILTING LINES

STRAIGHT FOLD

DIAGONAL FOLD

2

PINK GINGER

Remember to add 1/8" cutting allowance for hand appliqué.

1

PINK GINGER ©2004 Elizabeth Root · Friendship Quilts...the Hawaiian Way

CENTER

STRAIGHT FOLD

7"

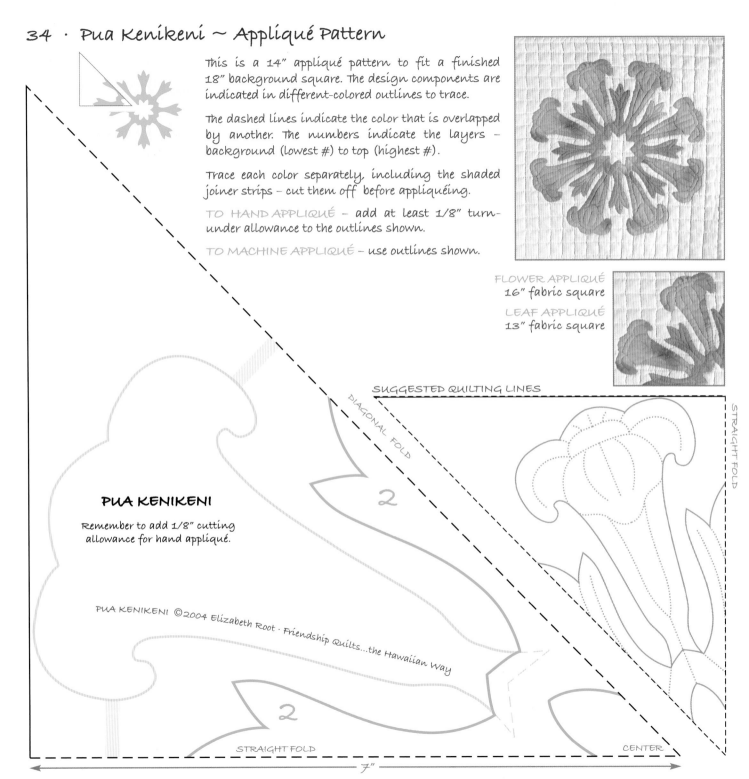

This is a 14" appliqué pattern to fit a finished 18" background square. The design components are indicated in different-colored outlines to trace.

The dashed lines indicate the color that is overlapped by another. The numbers indicate the layers – background (lowest #) to top (highest #).

Trace each color separately, including the shaded joiner strips – cut them off before appliquéing.

TO HAND APPLIQUÉ – add at least 1/8" turn-under allowance to the outlines shown.

TO MACHINE APPLIQUÉ – use outlines shown.

FLOWER APPLIQUÉ
16" fabric square

LEAF APPLIQUÉ
13" fabric square

SUGGESTED QUILTING LINES

DIAGONAL FOLD

STRAIGHT FOLD

PUA KENIKENI

Remember to add 1/8" cutting allowance for hand appliqué.

PUA KENIKENI ©2004 Elizabeth Root · Friendship Quilts...the Hawaiian Way

2

2

STRAIGHT FOLD

CENTER

7"

This is a 14" appliqué pattern to fit a finished 18" background square. The design components are indicated in different-colored outlines to trace.

The dashed lines indicate the color that is overlapped by another. The numbers indicate the layers – background (lowest #) to top (highest #).

Trace each color separately, including the shaded joiner strips – cut them off before appliquéing.

TO HAND APPLIQUÉ – add at least 1/8" turn-under allowance to the outlines shown.

TO MACHINE APPLIQUÉ – use outlines shown.

FLOWER APPLIQUÉ
14" fabric square

LEAF APPLIQUÉ
16" fabric square

SUGGESTED QUILTING LINES

STRAIGHT FOLD

DIAGONAL FOLD

1

SPIDERLILY

Remember to add 1/8" cutting allowance for hand appliqué.

2

2

SPIDERLILY ©2004 Elizabeth Root · Friendship Quilts...the Hawaiian Way

CENTER

STRAIGHT FOLD

7"

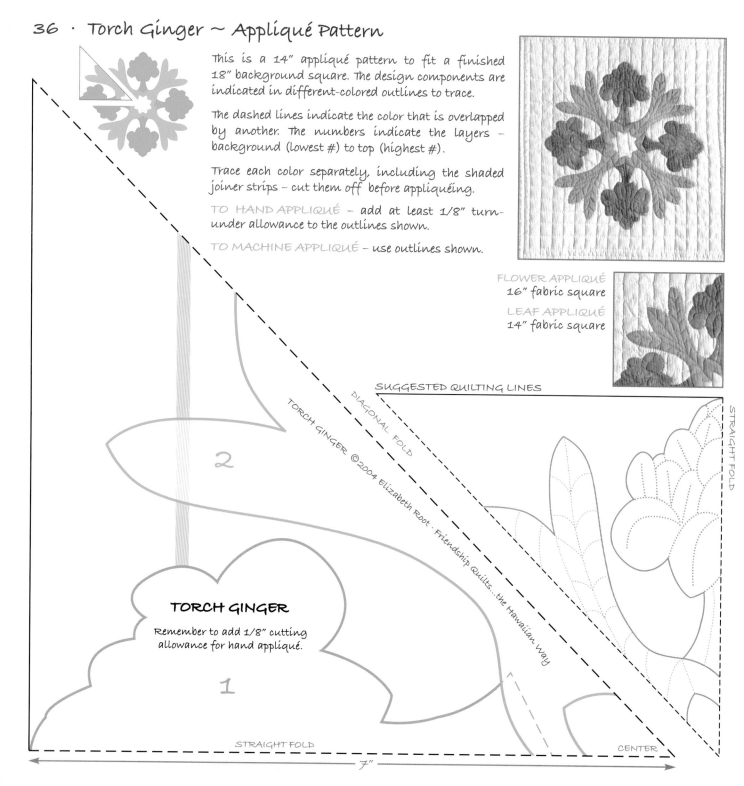

This is a 14" appliqué pattern to fit a finished 18" background square. The design components are indicated in different-colored outlines to trace.

The dashed lines indicate the color that is overlapped by another. The numbers indicate the layers – background (lowest #) to top (highest #).

Trace each color separately, including the shaded joiner strips – cut them off before appliquéing.

TO HAND APPLIQUÉ – add at least 1/8" turn-under allowance to the outlines shown.

TO MACHINE APPLIQUÉ – use outlines shown.

FLOWER APPLIQUÉ
16" fabric square

LEAF APPLIQUÉ
14" fabric square

SUGGESTED QUILTING LINES

DIAGONAL FOLD

STRAIGHT FOLD

TORCH GINGER ©2004 Elizabeth Root · Friendship Quilts...the Hawaiian Way

2

TORCH GINGER

Remember to add 1/8" cutting allowance for hand appliqué.

1

STRAIGHT FOLD

CENTER

7"

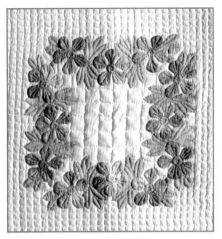

This is a 14" appliqué pattern to fit a finished 18" background square. The design components are indicated in different-colored outlines to trace.

The dashed lines indicate the color that is overlapped by another. The numbers indicate the layers – background (lowest #) to top (highest #).

Trace each color separately, including the shaded joiner strips – cut them off before appliquéing.

TO HAND APPLIQUÉ – add at least 1/8" turn-under allowance to the outlines shown.

TO MACHINE APPLIQUÉ – use outlines shown.

FLOWER APPLIQUÉ
16" fabric square
LEAF APPLIQUÉ
16" fabric square

*For Blue Flower Quilt (pp. 72-73), use 16" background square.

SUGGESTED QUILTING LINES

STRAIGHT FOLD

DIAGONAL FOLD

VINCA

Remember to add 1/8" cutting allowance for hand appliqué.

1

2

1

2

VINCA ©2004 Elizabeth Root ·
Friendship Quilts...the Hawaiian Way

CENTER

STRAIGHT FOLD

7"

This is a 30" appliqué pattern (the pattern below will need to be enlarged 150%) to fit a finished 36" background square. The design components are indicated in different-colored outlines to trace.

The dashed lines indicate the color that is overlapped by another. The numbers indicate the layers – background (lowest #) to top (highest #).

Trace each color separately, including the shaded joiner strips – cut them off when the appliqué has been positioned, pinned and/or basted.

HAND APPLIQUÉ – add at least 1/8" turn-under allowance to the outlines shown.

MACHINE APPLIQUÉ – use outlines shown.

FLOWER APPLIQUÉ
Large Flowers: 32" x 32"
To Hand Place: Cut four - 11" x 11"
Flower Center: Cut eight - 6" x 6"

Small Flowers: 32" x 32"
To Hand Place: Cut four - 5.5"x 5.5"
Flower Center: Cut eight - 3" x 3"

Flower center patterns on page 98

LEAF APPLIQUÉ
24" x 24"

The fabric allowances above are for the 30" appliqué pattern.

Remember to add 1/8" minimum turn-under allowance to the design outline if doing hand appliqué.

BORDER DETAIL

"Any day is sunny
that's brightened by a smile,
Any friendship blossoms
if it's tended with style."
~ unknown

CENTER DETAIL

10" to enlarge to 15" (150%)

If enlarging each page separately, use green bars to line up each side.

© 2004 Elizabeth Root · Friendship Quilts...the Hawaiian Way · GARDEN QUILT CENTER

STRAIGHT FOLD

DIAGONAL FOLD

Binding 1"

3"

16"

3"

10"

60"

When cutting the background, a 1/2" seam allowance should be added to each section.

60"

10"

QUILT BLOCK PATTERNS (left to right):
ROW 1: Maunaloa, 45; Yellow Ginger, 50; Ilima, 44;
ROW 2: Pikake, 47; Anthurium, 42; Tuberose, 49; ROW 3: Bougainvillea, 43; Rose, 48; Orchid, 46;
NINE-PATCH, 96; BORDER CORNER DESIGN, 90;
BORDER VINE DESIGN: end pattern, 91; three center sections, 92-93

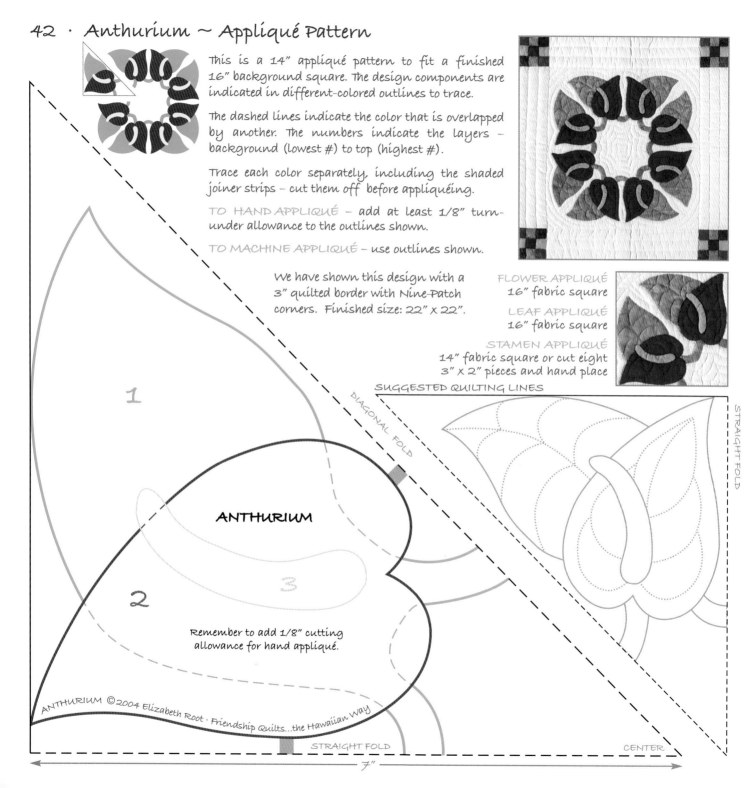

This is a 14" appliqué pattern to fit a finished 16" background square. The design components are indicated in different-colored outlines to trace.

The dashed lines indicate the color that is overlapped by another. The numbers indicate the layers – background (lowest #) to top (highest #).

Trace each color separately, including the shaded joiner strips – cut them off before appliquéing.

TO HAND APPLIQUÉ – add at least 1/8" turn-under allowance to the outlines shown.

TO MACHINE APPLIQUÉ – use outlines shown.

We have shown this design with a 3" quilted border with Nine-Patch corners. Finished size: 22" x 22".

FLOWER APPLIQUÉ
16" fabric square

LEAF APPLIQUÉ
16" fabric square

STAMEN APPLIQUÉ
14" fabric square or cut eight
3" x 2" pieces and hand place

SUGGESTED QUILTING LINES

DIAGONAL FOLD

STRAIGHT FOLD

1

ANTHURIUM

2

3

Remember to add 1/8" cutting allowance for hand appliqué.

ANTHURIUM ©2004 Elizabeth Root · Friendship Quilts...the Hawaiian Way

STRAIGHT FOLD

CENTER

7"

This is a 14" appliqué pattern to fit a finished 16" background square. The design components are indicated in different-colored outlines to trace.

The dashed lines indicate the color that is overlapped by another. The numbers indicate the layers – background (lowest #) to top (highest #).

Trace each color separately, including the shaded joiner strips – cut them off before appliquéing.

TO HAND APPLIQUÉ – add at least 1/8" turn-under allowance to the outlines shown.

TO MACHINE APPLIQUÉ – use outlines shown.

FLOWER APPLIQUÉ
12" fabric square

LEAF APPLIQUÉ
16" fabric square

EMBROIDERY
Hand embroider centers of flowers with french knots and chain stitch

We have shown this design with a 3" quilted border with Nine-Patch corners. Finished size: 22" x 22".

SUGGESTED QUILTING LINES

STRAIGHT FOLD

DIAGONAL FOLD

CENTER

STRAIGHT FOLD

1

2

1

BOUGAINVILLEA

Remember to add 1/8" cutting allowance for hand appliqué.

BOUGAINVILLEA ©2004 Elizabeth Root · Friendship Quilts...the Hawaiian Way

7"

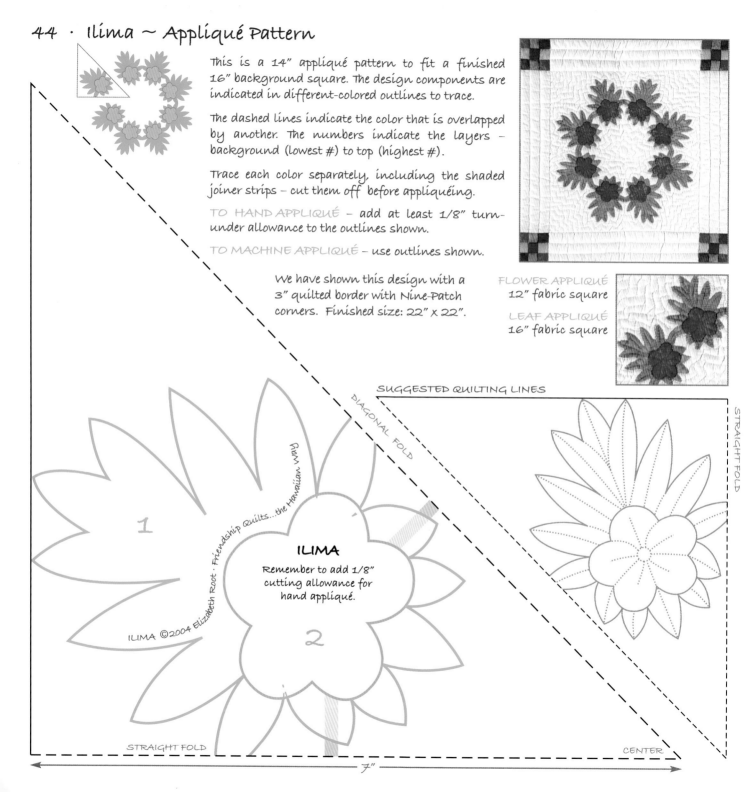

This is a 14" appliqué pattern to fit a finished 16" background square. The design components are indicated in different-colored outlines to trace.

The dashed lines indicate the color that is overlapped by another. The numbers indicate the layers – background (lowest #) to top (highest #).

Trace each color separately, including the shaded joiner strips – cut them off before appliquéing.

TO HAND APPLIQUÉ – add at least 1/8" turn-under allowance to the outlines shown.

TO MACHINE APPLIQUÉ – use outlines shown.

We have shown this design with a 3" quilted border with Nine-Patch corners. Finished size: 22" x 22".

FLOWER APPLIQUÉ
12" fabric square

LEAF APPLIQUÉ
16" fabric square

SUGGESTED QUILTING LINES

DIAGONAL FOLD

STRAIGHT FOLD

1

ILIMA ©2004 Elizabeth Root · Friendship Quilts...the Hawaiian Way

ILIMA

Remember to add 1/8" cutting allowance for hand appliqué.

2

STRAIGHT FOLD

CENTER

7"

This is a 14" appliqué pattern to fit a finished 16" background square. The design components are indicated in different-colored outlines to trace.

The dashed lines indicate the color that is overlapped by another. The numbers indicate the layers – background (lowest #) to top (highest #).

Trace each color separately, including the shaded joiner strips – cut them off before appliquéing.

TO HAND APPLIQUÉ – add at least 1/8" turn-under allowance to the outlines shown.

TO MACHINE APPLIQUÉ – use outlines shown.

FLOWER APPLIQUÉ
12" fabric square

LEAF APPLIQUÉ
16" fabric square

We have shown this design with a 3" quilted border with Nine-Patch corners. Finished size: 22" x 22".

SUGGESTED QUILTING LINES

STRAIGHT FOLD

DIAGONAL FOLD

1

MAUNALOA ©2004 Elizabeth Root ·
Friendship Quilts...the Hawaiian Way

MAUNALOA
Remember to add 1/8"
cutting allowance for
hand appliqué.

2

1

CENTER

STRAIGHT FOLD

7"

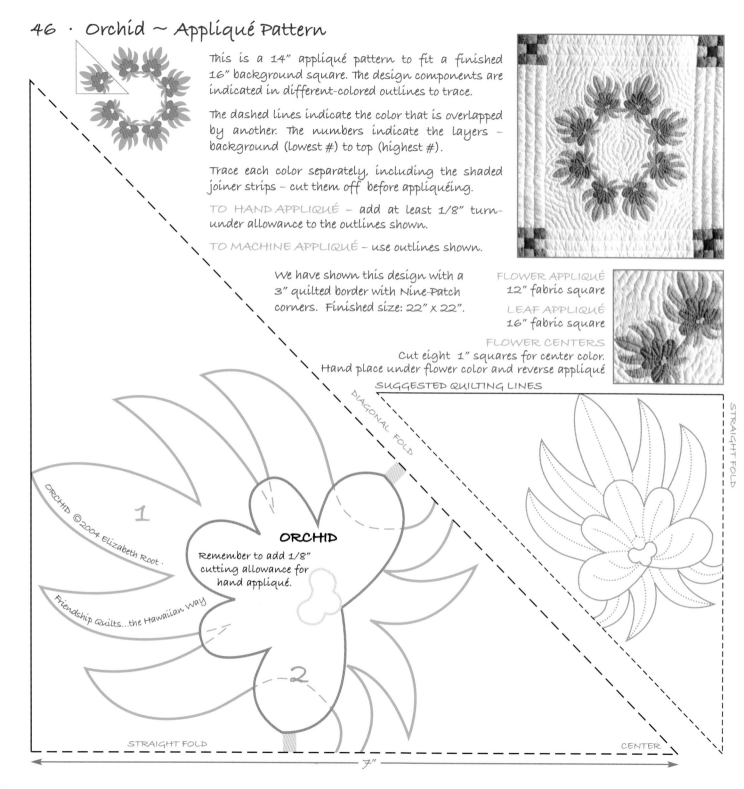

This is a 14" appliqué pattern to fit a finished 16" background square. The design components are indicated in different-colored outlines to trace.

The dashed lines indicate the color that is overlapped by another. The numbers indicate the layers – background (lowest #) to top (highest #).

Trace each color separately, including the shaded joiner strips – cut them off before appliquéing.

TO HAND APPLIQUÉ – add at least 1/8" turn-under allowance to the outlines shown.

TO MACHINE APPLIQUÉ – use outlines shown.

We have shown this design with a 3" quilted border with Nine-Patch corners. Finished size: 22" x 22".

FLOWER APPLIQUÉ
12" fabric square

LEAF APPLIQUÉ
16" fabric square

FLOWER CENTERS
Cut eight 1" squares for center color.
Hand place under flower color and reverse appliqué

SUGGESTED QUILTING LINES

DIAGONAL FOLD

STRAIGHT FOLD

ORCHID

Remember to add 1/8" cutting allowance for hand appliqué.

1

2

ORCHID ©2004 Elizabeth Root

Friendship Quilts...the Hawaiian Way

STRAIGHT FOLD

CENTER

7"

This is a 14" appliqué pattern to fit a finished 16" background square. The design components are indicated in different-colored outlines to trace.

The dashed lines indicate the color that is overlapped by another. The numbers indicate the layers – background (lowest #) to top (highest #).

Trace each color separately, including the shaded joiner strips – cut them off before appliquéing.

TO HAND APPLIQUÉ – add at least 1/8" turn-under allowance to the outlines shown.

TO MACHINE APPLIQUÉ – use outlines shown.

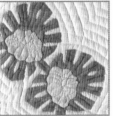

FLOWER APPLIQUÉ
12" fabric square

LEAF APPLIQUÉ
16" fabric square

We have shown this design with a 3" quilted border with Nine-Patch corners. Finished size: 22" x 22".

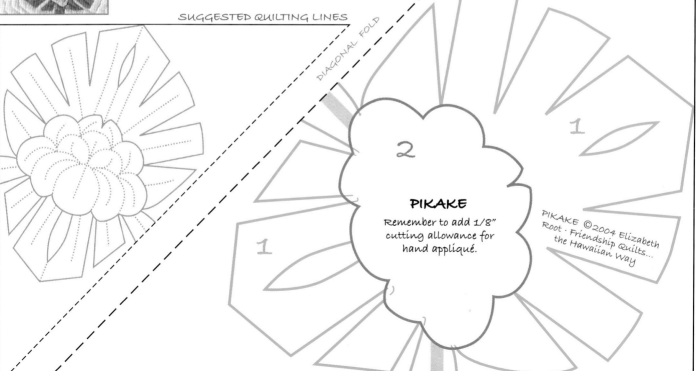

SUGGESTED QUILTING LINES

STRAIGHT FOLD

DIAGONAL FOLD

CENTER

STRAIGHT FOLD

PIKAKE

Remember to add 1/8" cutting allowance for hand appliqué.

1

2

1

PIKAKE ©2004 Elizabeth Root · Friendship Quilts... the Hawaiian Way

7"

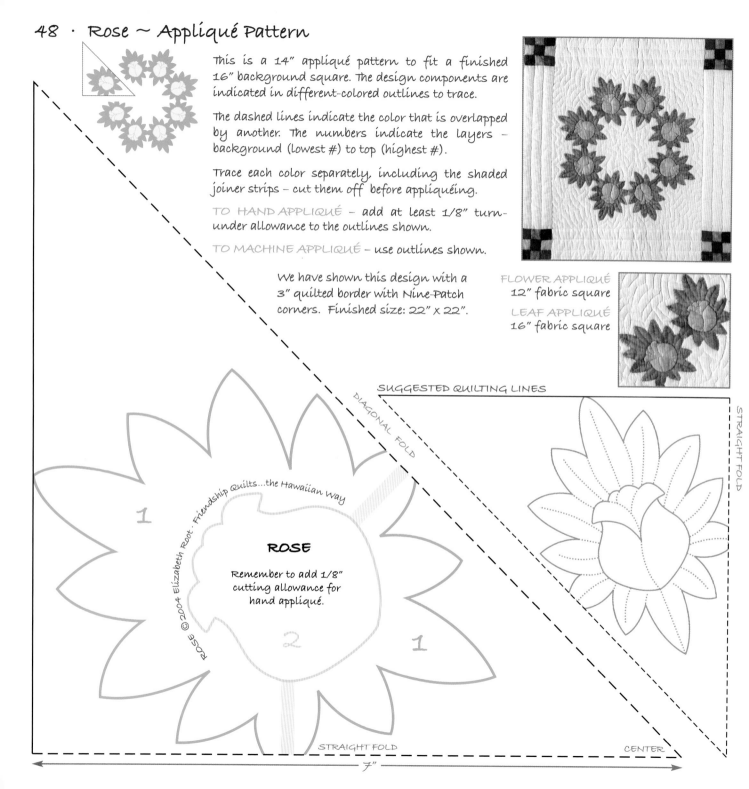

This is a 14" appliqué pattern to fit a finished 16" background square. The design components are indicated in different-colored outlines to trace.

The dashed lines indicate the color that is overlapped by another. The numbers indicate the layers – background (lowest #) to top (highest #).

Trace each color separately, including the shaded joiner strips – cut them off before appliquéing.

TO HAND APPLIQUÉ – add at least 1/8" turn-under allowance to the outlines shown.

TO MACHINE APPLIQUÉ – use outlines shown.

We have shown this design with a 3" quilted border with Nine-Patch corners. Finished size: 22" x 22".

FLOWER APPLIQUÉ
12" fabric square

LEAF APPLIQUÉ
16" fabric square

SUGGESTED QUILTING LINES

DIAGONAL FOLD

STRAIGHT FOLD

ROSE © 2004 Elizabeth Root. Friendship Quilts...the Hawaiian Way

ROSE

Remember to add 1/8" cutting allowance for hand appliqué.

1

2

1

STRAIGHT FOLD

CENTER

7"

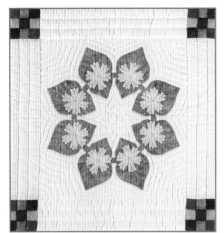

This is a 14" appliqué pattern to fit a finished 16" background square. The design components are indicated in different-colored outlines to trace.

The dashed lines indicate the color that is overlapped by another. The numbers indicate the layers – background (lowest #) to top (highest #).

Trace each color separately, including the shaded joiner strips – cut them off before appliquéing.

TO HAND APPLIQUÉ – add at least 1/8" turn-under allowance to the outlines shown.

TO MACHINE APPLIQUÉ – use outlines shown.

FLOWER APPLIQUÉ
12" fabric square

LEAF APPLIQUÉ
16" fabric square

We have shown this design with a 3" quilted border with Nine-Patch corners. Finished size: 22" x 22".

SUGGESTED QUILTING LINES

STRAIGHT FOLD

DIAGONAL FOLD

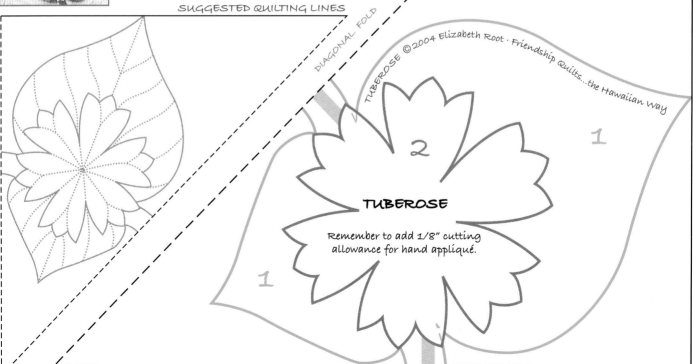

2

1

1

TUBEROSE

Remember to add 1/8" cutting allowance for hand appliqué.

CENTER

STRAIGHT FOLD

7"

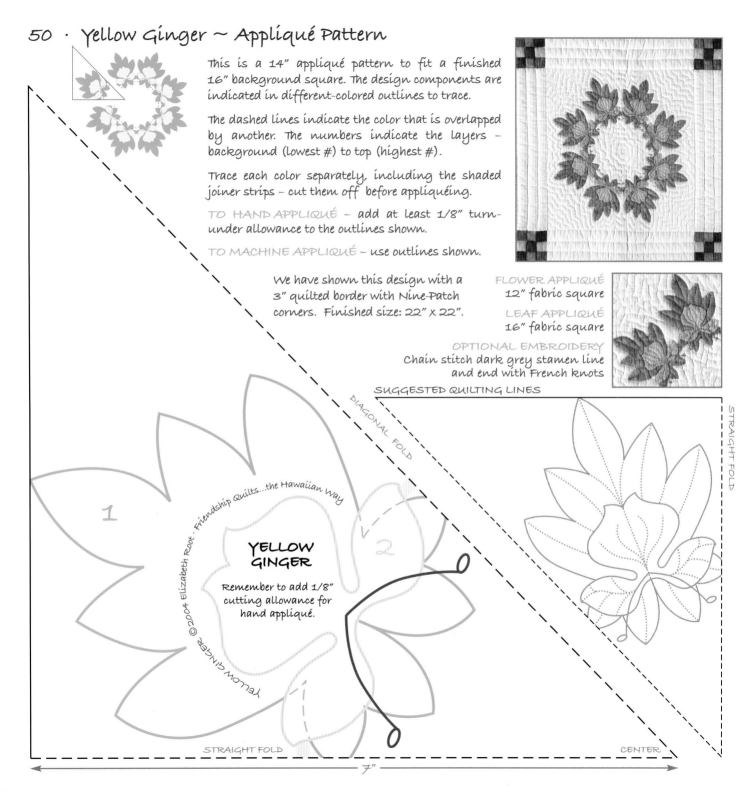

This is a 14" appliqué pattern to fit a finished 16" background square. The design components are indicated in different-colored outlines to trace.

The dashed lines indicate the color that is overlapped by another. The numbers indicate the layers – background (lowest #) to top (highest #).

Trace each color separately, including the shaded joiner strips – cut them off before appliquéing.

TO HAND APPLIQUÉ – add at least 1/8" turn-under allowance to the outlines shown.

TO MACHINE APPLIQUÉ – use outlines shown.

We have shown this design with a 3" quilted border with Nine-Patch corners. Finished size: 22" x 22".

FLOWER APPLIQUÉ
12" fabric square

LEAF APPLIQUÉ
16" fabric square

OPTIONAL EMBROIDERY
Chain stitch dark grey stamen line and end with French knots

SUGGESTED QUILTING LINES

DIAGONAL FOLD

STRAIGHT FOLD

1

2

© 2004 Elizabeth Root · Friendship Quilts...the Hawaiian Way

YELLOW GINGER

Remember to add 1/8" cutting allowance for hand appliqué.

YELLOW GINGER

STRAIGHT FOLD

CENTER

7"

The Friendship Portulaca Quilt is a good example of manipulating one quilt pattern to make nine. The full size patterns for the designs below are found on their listed pages. All of the appliqué patterns in this quilt are 15" square, except the center, which is 10" x 10". All are on 20" x 20" finished backgrounds.

QUILT BLOCKS WITH LARGE FLOWERS NEAR THE OUTSIDE EDGE
Large Flowers: 17" x 17"   To Hand Place: Cut 8 - 6" x 6" Center: 3" x 3"
Small Flowers: 17" x 17"   To Hand Place: Cut 16 - 3"x 3"   Center: 1.5" x 1.5"

QUILT BLOCKS WITH LARGE FLOWERS NEAR THE CENTER
Large Flowers: 12" x 12"   To Hand Place: Cut 8 - 6" x 6" Center: 3" x 3"
Small Flowers: 17" x 17"   To Hand Place: Cut 16 - 3"x 3"   Center: 1.5" x 1.5"

LEAVES / Leaves only: 7" x 7"

• = center of pattern

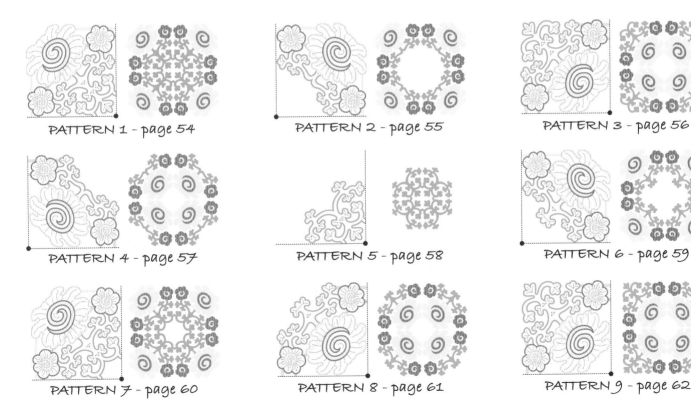

PATTERN 1 - page 54   PATTERN 2 - page 55   PATTERN 3 - page 56

PATTERN 4 - page 57   PATTERN 5 - page 58   PATTERN 6 - page 59

PATTERN 7 - page 60   PATTERN 8 - page 61   PATTERN 9 - page 62

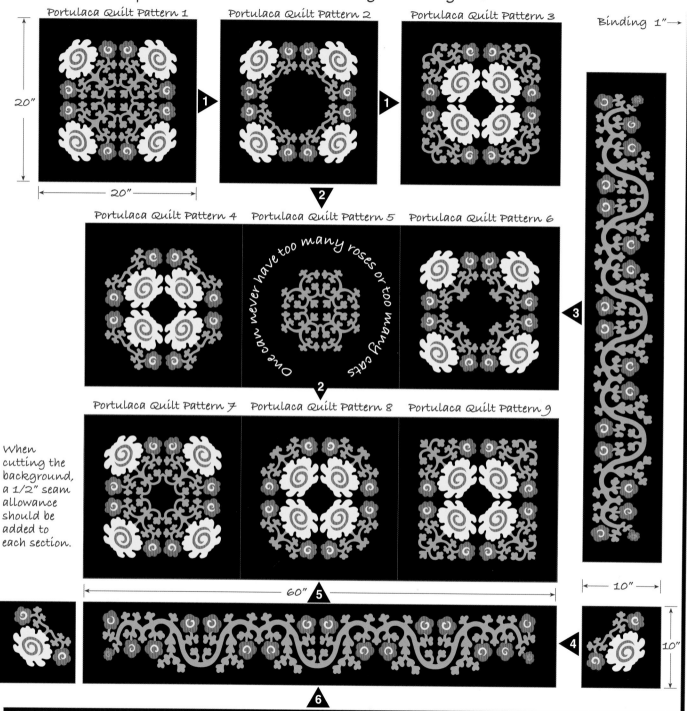

Portulaca Quilt Pattern 1

Portulaca Quilt Pattern 2

Portulaca Quilt Pattern 3

20"

20"

Binding 1"→

Portulaca Quilt Pattern 4

Portulaca Quilt Pattern 5

Portulaca Quilt Pattern 6

One can never have too many roses or too many cats

Portulaca Quilt Pattern 7

Portulaca Quilt Pattern 8

Portulaca Quilt Pattern 9

When cutting the background, a 1/2" seam allowance should be added to each section.

60"

10"

10"

81"

DESIGN IDENTIFICATION AND PATTERN PAGES, 51;
BORDER CORNER DESIGN, 55; CENTER DESIGN, 58;
BORDER VINE DESIGN: End pattern, 93; three center sections, 94-95

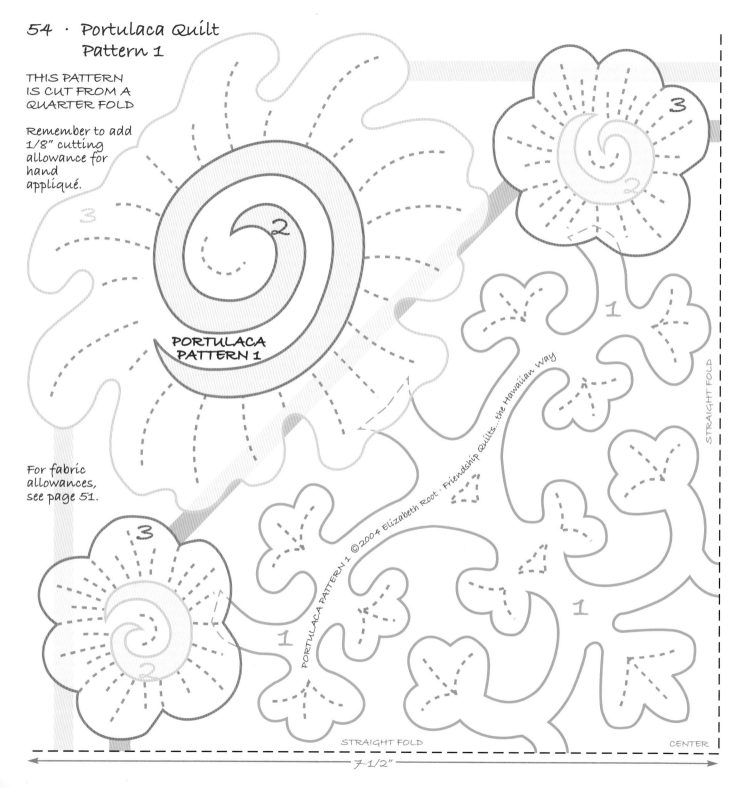

54 · Portulaca Quilt
Pattern 1

THIS PATTERN
IS CUT FROM A
QUARTER FOLD

Remember to add
1/8" cutting
allowance for
hand
appliqué.

For fabric
allowances,
see page 51.

PORTULACA
PATTERN 1

3

2

3

2

2

3

1

1

1

PORTULACA PATTERN 1 ©2004 Elizabeth Root · Friendship Quilts...the Hawaiian Way

STRAIGHT FOLD

STRAIGHT FOLD

CENTER

7-1/2"

THIS PATTERN IS
CUT FROM A
QUARTER FOLD

3

2

PORTULACA
PATTERN 2

PORTULACA PATTERN 2 ©2004 Elizabeth Root · Friendship Quilts...the Hawaiian Way

1

3

1

2

STRAIGHT FOLD

Remember to add
1/8" cutting
allowance for
hand appliqué.

For fabric
allowances,
see page 51.

CENTER

STRAIGHT FOLD

7-1/2"

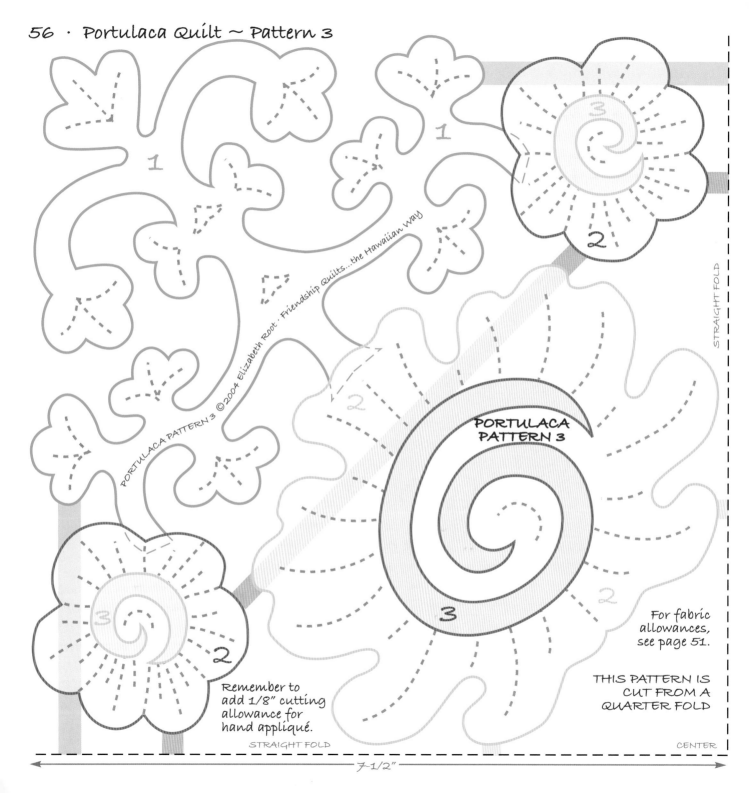

PORTULACA
PATTERN 3

PORTULACA PATTERN 3 ©2004 Elizabeth Root · Friendship Quilts...the Hawaiian Way

Remember to
add 1/8" cutting
allowance for
hand appliqué.

For fabric
allowances,
see page 51.

THIS PATTERN IS
CUT FROM A
QUARTER FOLD

STRAIGHT FOLD

STRAIGHT FOLD

CENTER

7-1/2"

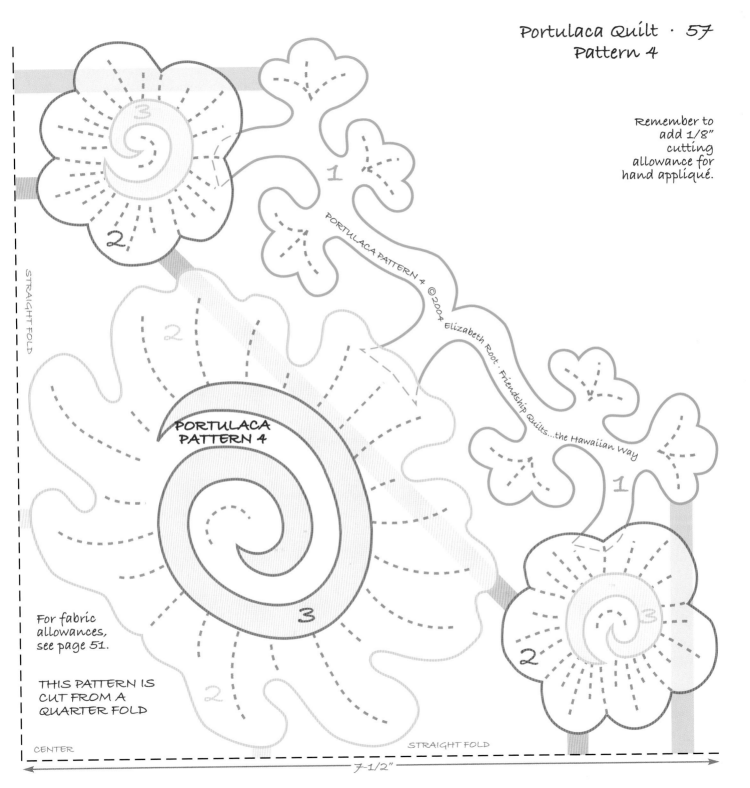

Remember to
add 1/8"
cutting
allowance for
hand appliqué.

PORTULACA PATTERN 4 © 2004 Elizabeth Root · Friendship Quilts...the Hawaiian Way

STRAIGHT FOLD

PORTULACA
PATTERN 4

For fabric
allowances,
see page 51.

THIS PATTERN IS
CUT FROM A
QUARTER FOLD

CENTER

STRAIGHT FOLD

7-1/2"

58 · Portulaca Quilt
Pattern 5

THIS PATTERN IS CUT
FROM A QUARTER FOLD

Remember to add 1/8"
cutting allowance for
hand appliqué.

For fabric allowances,
see page 51.

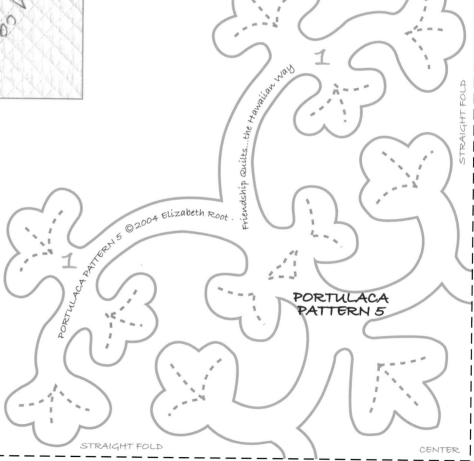

PORTULACA PATTERN 5 ©2004 Elizabeth Root .

Friendship Quilts...the Hawaiian Way

1

1

PORTULACA
PATTERN 5

STRAIGHT FOLD

STRAIGHT FOLD

CENTER

5"

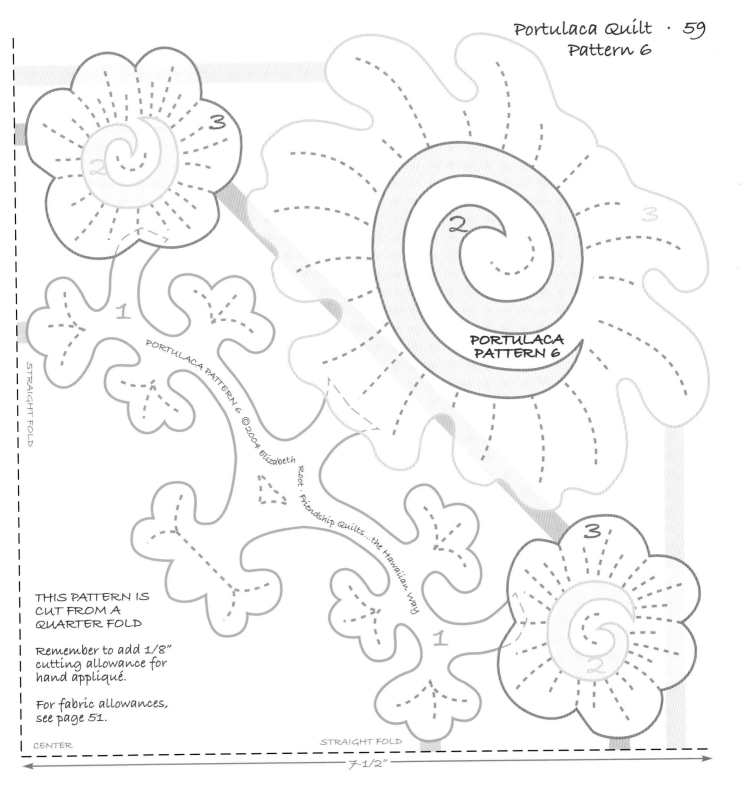

3

2

1

2

3

PORTULACA
PATTERN 6

PORTULACA PATTERN 6 ©2004 Elizabeth Root · Friendship Quilts...the Hawaiian Way

3

1

2

STRAIGHT FOLD

THIS PATTERN IS
CUT FROM A
QUARTER FOLD

Remember to add 1/8"
cutting allowance for
hand appliqué.

For fabric allowances,
see page 51.

CENTER

STRAIGHT FOLD

7-1/2"

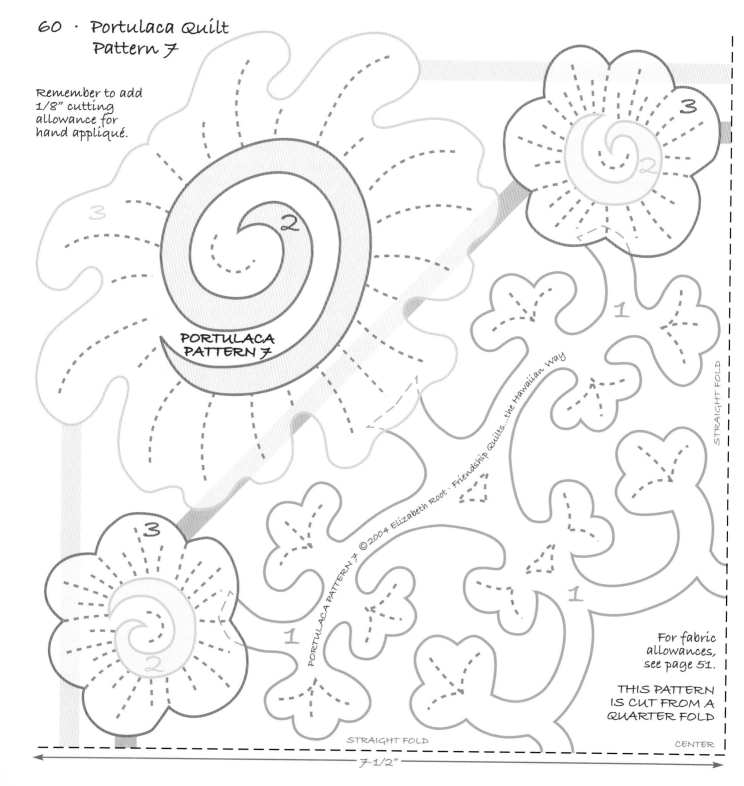

60 · Portulaca Quilt
Pattern 7

Remember to add
1/8" cutting
allowance for
hand appliqué.

PORTULACA
PATTERN 7

PORTULACA PATTERN 7 ©2004 Elizabeth Root : Friendship Quilts...the Hawaiian Way

STRAIGHT FOLD

For fabric
allowances,
see page 51.

THIS PATTERN
IS CUT FROM A
QUARTER FOLD

STRAIGHT FOLD

CENTER

7-1/2"

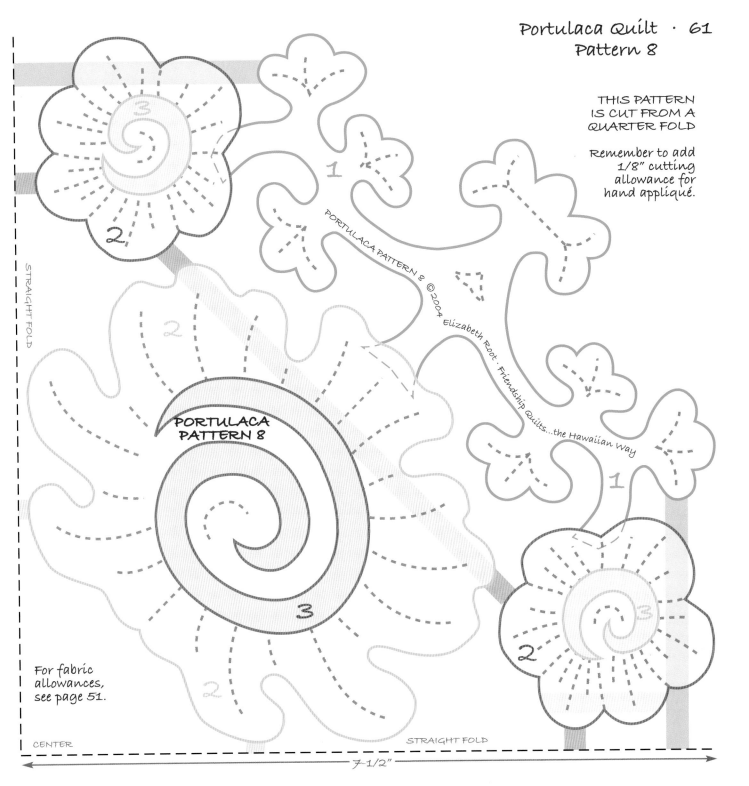

THIS PATTERN
IS CUT FROM A
QUARTER FOLD

Remember to add
1/8" cutting
allowance for
hand appliqué.

PORTULACA PATTERN 8 © 2004 Elizabeth Root · Friendship Quilts...the Hawaiian Way

STRAIGHT FOLD

3

2

1

2

PORTULACA
PATTERN 8

3

2

1

3

2

For fabric
allowances,
see page 51.

CENTER

STRAIGHT FOLD

7-1/2"

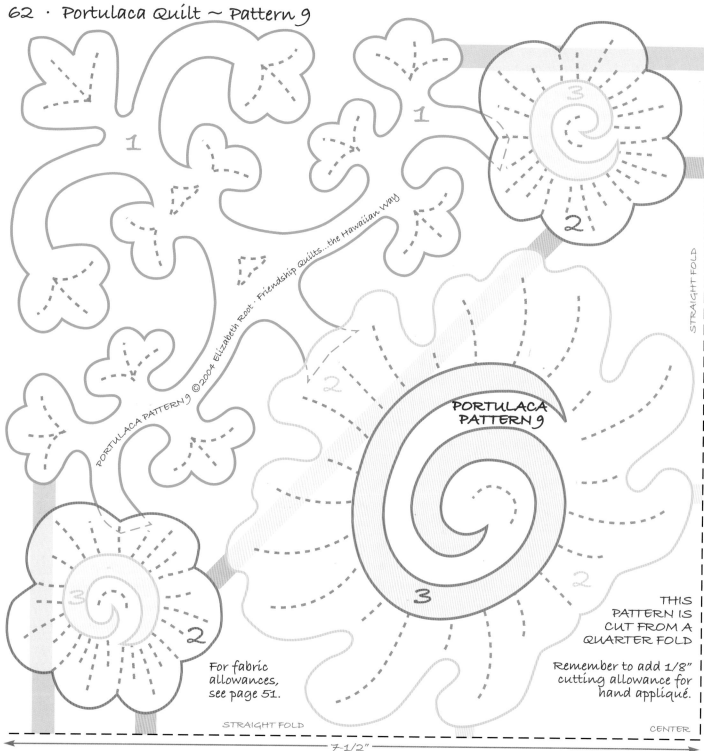

PORTULACA PATTERN 9 ©2004 Elizabeth Root · Friendship Quilts...the Hawaiian Way

PORTULACA
PATTERN 9

For fabric
allowances,
see page 51.

THIS
PATTERN IS
CUT FROM A
QUARTER FOLD

Remember to add 1/8"
cutting allowance for
hand appliqué.

STRAIGHT FOLD

CENTER

STRAIGHT FOLD

7-1/2"

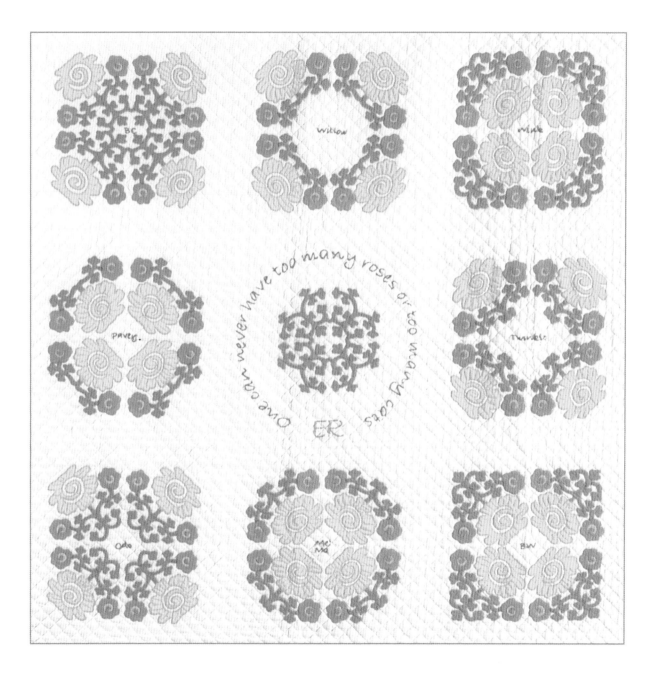

"Come and visit me, my friend...my flowers would like to meet you."
~ Unknown

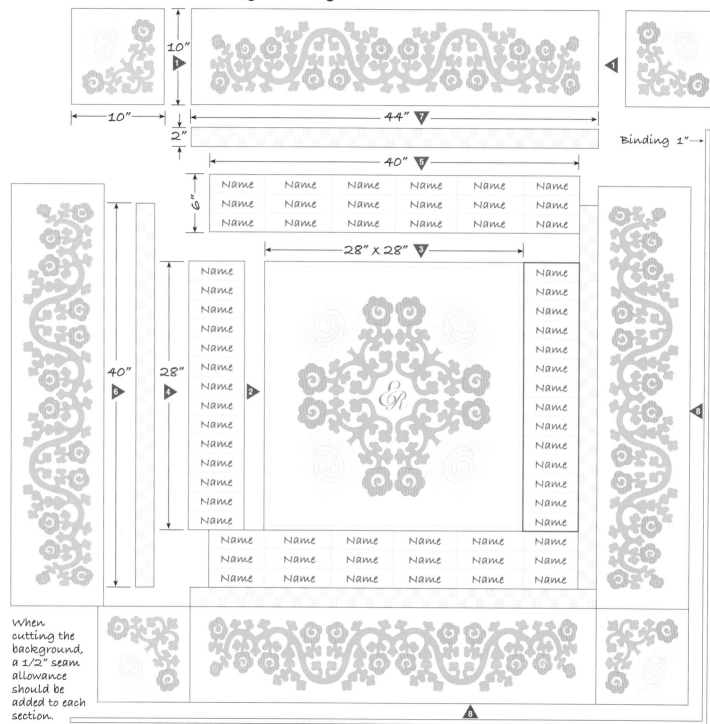

10"

10"

2"

44" 7

Binding 1"→

40" 5

6"

Name	Name	Name	Name	Name	Name
Name	Name	Name	Name	Name	Name
Name	Name	Name	Name	Name	Name

28" x 28" 3

40"

28"

6

4

2

8

Name					Name
Name					Name
Name					Name
Name					Name
Name					Name
Name					Name
Name	ER				Name
Name					Name
Name					Name
Name					Name
Name					Name
Name					Name
Name					Name

Name	Name	Name	Name	Name	Name
Name	Name	Name	Name	Name	Name
Name	Name	Name	Name	Name	Name

When cutting the background, a 1/2" seam allowance should be added to each section.

8

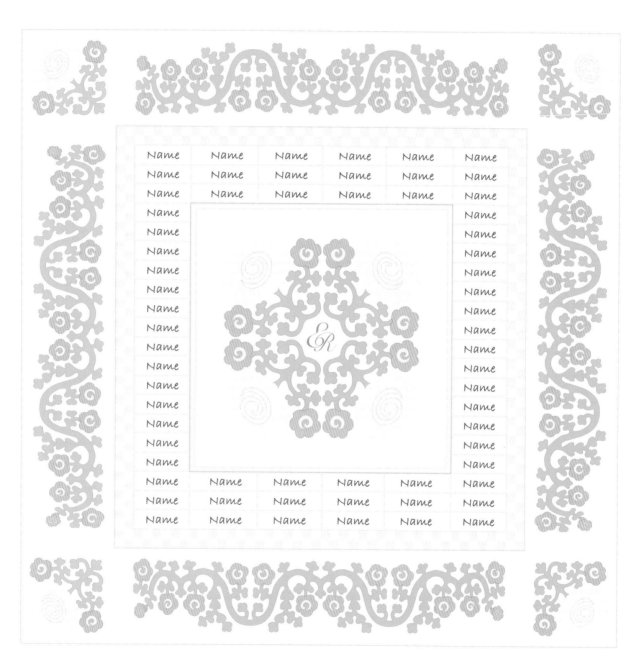

CENTER DESIGN PATTERN, 66-67;
BORDER CORNER DESIGN, 90;
BORDER VINE DESIGN: end pattern, 91; two center sections, 92-93

This is a 21" appliqué pattern to fit a finished 28" background square. The design components are indicated in different-colored outlines to trace.

The dashed lines indicate the color that is overlapped by another. The numbers indicate the layers - background (lowest #) to top (highest #).

Trace each color separately, including the shaded joiner strips - cut them off when the appliqué has been positioned, pinned and/or basted.

HAND APPLIQUÉ - add at least 1/8" turn-under allowance to the outlines shown.

MACHINE APPLIQUÉ - use outlines shown.

FLOWER APPLIQUÉ
Large Flowers: 23" x 23"
To Hand Place: Cut four - 7" x 9"
Flower Center: Cut four - 4" x 5"

Small Flowers: 23" x 23"
To Hand Place: Cut eight - 4" x 5"
Flower Center: Cut eight - 2" x 2.5"

Flower center patterns
on page 98

LEAF APPLIQUÉ
18" x 18"

Remember to add
1/8" minimum
turn-under
allowance to the
design outline if
doing hand appliqué.

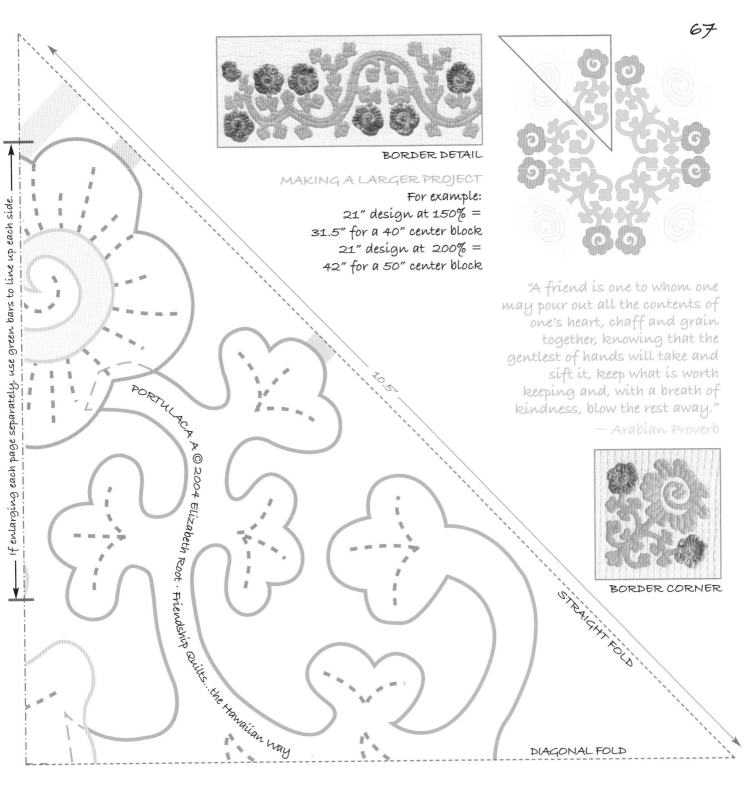

BORDER DETAIL

MAKING A LARGER PROJECT

For example:
21" design at 150% =
31.5" for a 40" center block
21" design at 200% =
42" for a 50" center block

"A friend is one to whom one may pour out all the contents of one's heart, chaff and grain together, knowing that the gentlest of hands will take and sift it, keep what is worth keeping and, with a breath of kindness, blow the rest away."

~ Arabian Proverb

BORDER CORNER

If enlarging each page separately, use green bars to line up each side.

PORTULACA A © 2004 Elizabeth Root · Friendship Quilts...the Hawaiian Way

10.5"

STRAIGHT FOLD

DIAGONAL FOLD

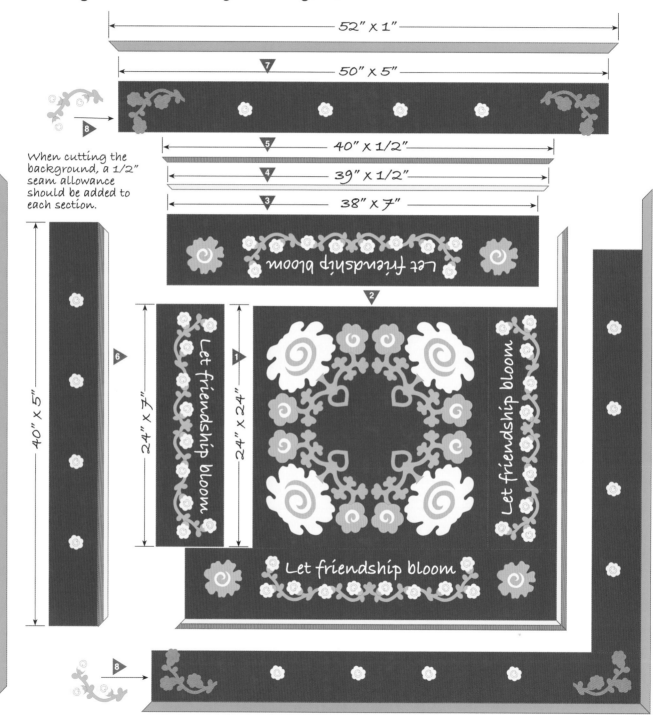

When cutting the background, a 1/2" seam allowance should be added to each section.

CENTER DESIGN PATTERN, 70-71; FLOWER GARLAND, 94-95;
CORNER OUTER BORDER DESIGN, 94-95; SINGLE FLOWERS, 98

This is a 20" appliqué pattern to fit a finished 24" background square. The design components are indicated in different-colored outlines to trace.

The dashed lines indicate the color that is overlapped by another. The numbers indicate the layers – background (lowest #) to top (highest #).

Trace each color separately, including the shaded joiner strips – cut them off when the appliqué has been positioned, pinned and/or basted.

HAND APPLIQUÉ – add at least 1/8" turn-under allowance to the outlines shown.

MACHINE APPLIQUÉ – use outlines shown.

FLOWER APPLIQUÉ
Large Flowers: 23" x 23"
To Hand Place: Cut four - 7" x 9"
Flower Center: Cut four - 4" x 5"

Small Flowers: 23" x 23"
To Hand Place: Cut eight - 4"x 5"
Flower Center: Cut eight - 2" x 2.5"

Flower center patterns on page 98

LEAF APPLIQUÉ
18" x 18"

Remember to add 1/8" minimum turn-under allowance to the design outline if doing hand appliqué.

BORDER DETAIL

MAKING A LARGER PROJECT

For example:

21" design at 150% =
31.5" for a 40" center block
21" design at 200% =
42" for a 50" center block

"May there always be work for your hands to do, may your purse always hold a coin or two. May the sun always shine on your windowpane, may a rainbow be certain to follow each rain. May the hand of a friend always be near you, may God fill your heart with gladness to cheer you."

~ Unknown

CORNER DETAIL

If enlarging each page separately, use green bars to line up each side.

PORTULACA B © 2004 Elizabeth Root · Friendship Quilts...the Hawaiian Way

10.5"

STRAIGHT FOLD

DIAGONAL FOLD

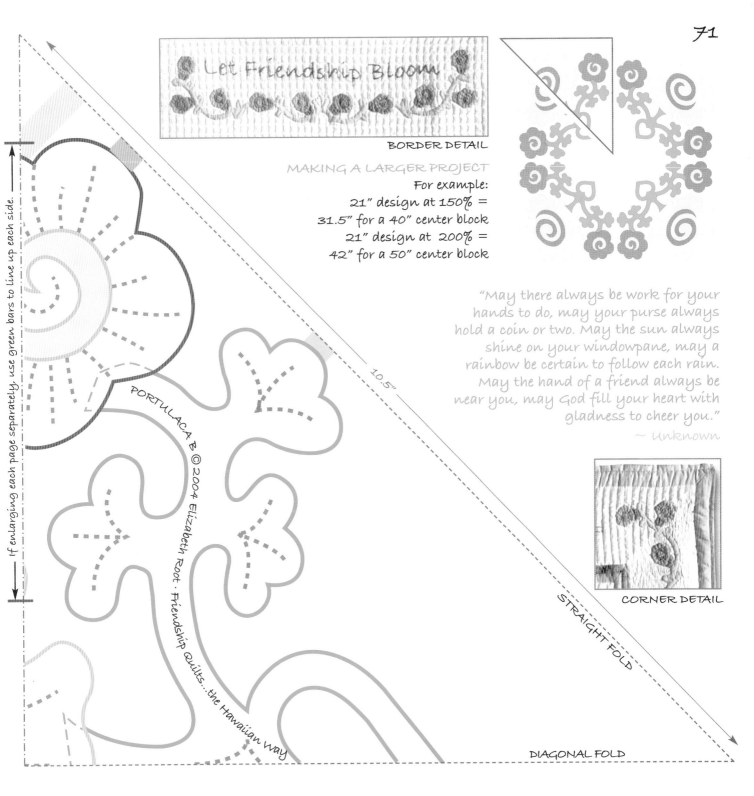

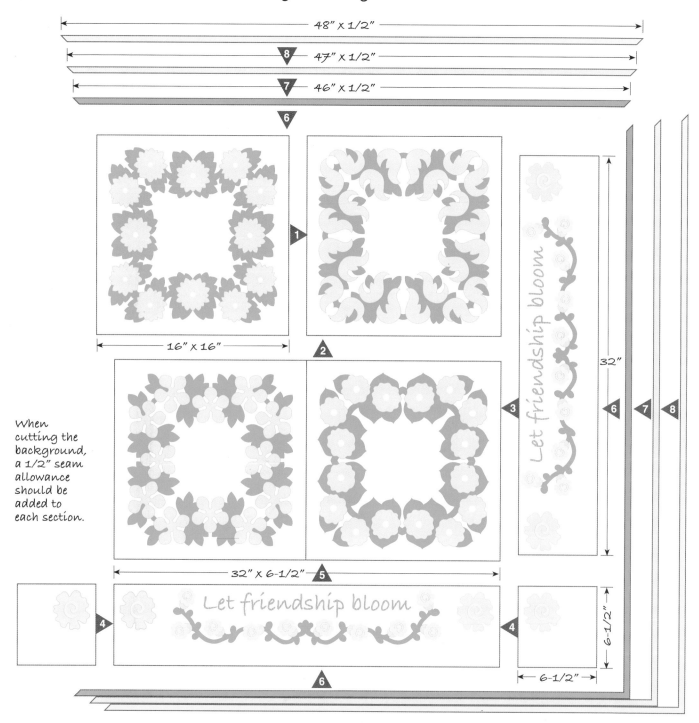

48" x 1/2"

8 47" x 1/2"

7 46" x 1/2"

6

16" x 16"

1

2

Let friendship bloom

3 6 7 8

32"

When cutting the background, a 1/2" seam allowance should be added to each section.

32" x 6-1/2" 5

6-1/2"

Let friendship bloom

4 4

6 6-1/2"

QUILT BLOCK DESIGNS: Passion Flower, 32; Blue Jade, 28; Vinca, 37; Morning Glory, 31
FLOWER GARLAND, 94-96; INDIVIDUAL FLOWERS, 98

3.75"

18"

18"

36"

6"

When cutting the background, a 1/2" seam allowance should be added to each section.

Nine-Patch pattern page 96

Scallop pattern page 97

Flower pattern page 98

Betty Bradley

Diana Wilson

Stacey Wilkinson

Petra Wiesnewski

Susanne Fonseca

Maria Gonzales

Elsa Jorgensen

Eloíse Parker-James

Valerie McDermott

Patty Hong

Mary Jones

Allyce Morgan

QUILT BLOCK DESIGNS (top left to bottom right):
Tahitian Gardenia, 79; Star Flower, 78; Orchid, 76; Plumeria, 77

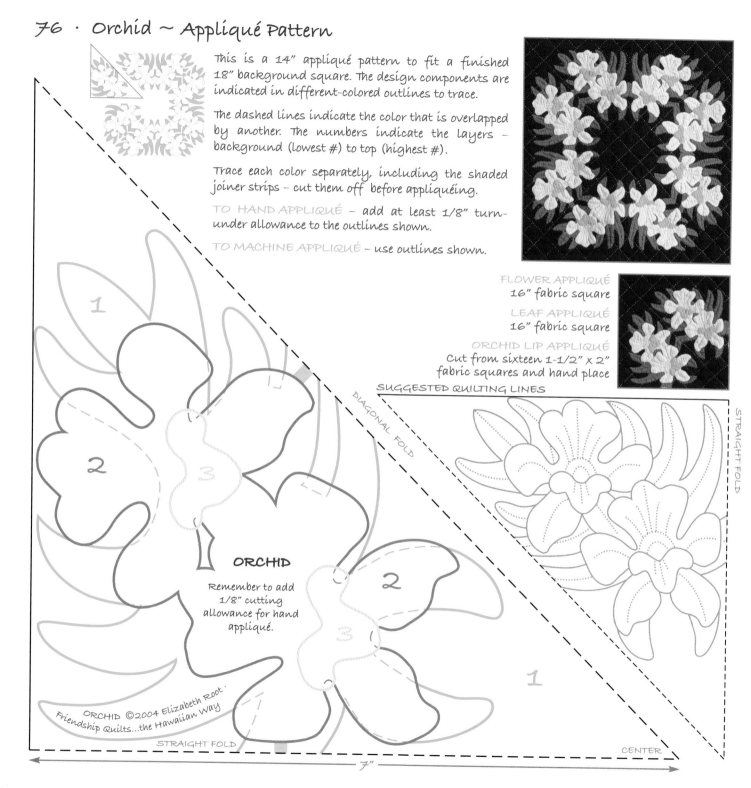

This is a 14" appliqué pattern to fit a finished 18" background square. The design components are indicated in different-colored outlines to trace.

The dashed lines indicate the color that is overlapped by another. The numbers indicate the layers – background (lowest #) to top (highest #).

Trace each color separately, including the shaded joiner strips – cut them off before appliquéing.

TO HAND APPLIQUÉ – add at least 1/8" turn-under allowance to the outlines shown.

TO MACHINE APPLIQUÉ – use outlines shown.

FLOWER APPLIQUÉ
16" fabric square

LEAF APPLIQUÉ
16" fabric square

ORCHID LIP APPLIQUÉ
Cut from sixteen 1-1/2" x 2"
fabric squares and hand place

SUGGESTED QUILTING LINES

DIAGONAL FOLD

STRAIGHT FOLD

ORCHID

Remember to add 1/8" cutting allowance for hand appliqué.

1

2

3

2

3

1

ORCHID ©2004 Elizabeth Root
Friendship Quilts...the Hawaiian Way

STRAIGHT FOLD

CENTER

7"

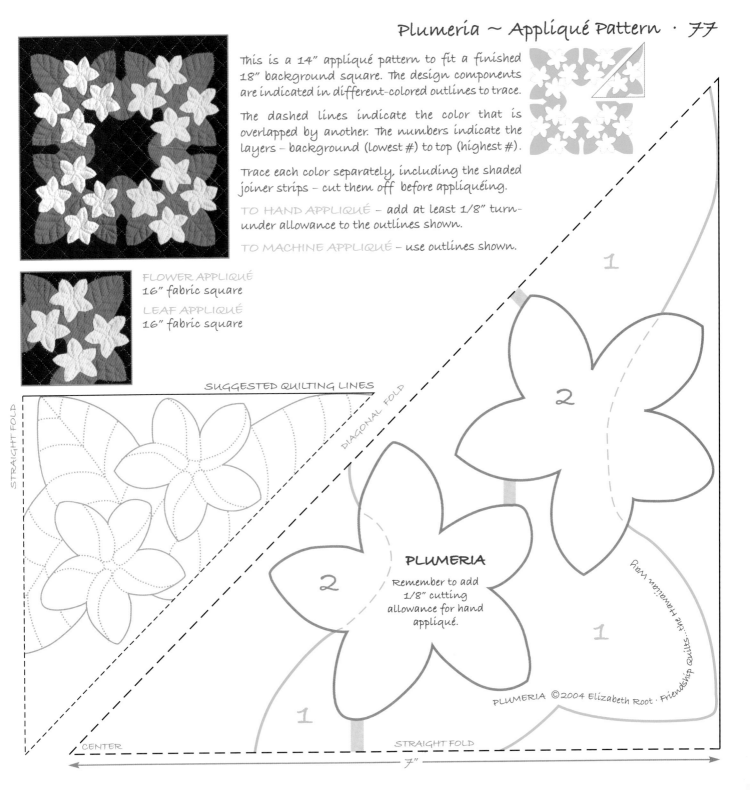

This is a 14" appliqué pattern to fit a finished 18" background square. The design components are indicated in different-colored outlines to trace.

The dashed lines indicate the color that is overlapped by another. The numbers indicate the layers – background (lowest #) to top (highest #).

Trace each color separately, including the shaded joiner strips – cut them off before appliquéing.

TO HAND APPLIQUÉ – add at least 1/8" turn-under allowance to the outlines shown.

TO MACHINE APPLIQUÉ – use outlines shown.

FLOWER APPLIQUÉ
16" fabric square

LEAF APPLIQUÉ
16" fabric square

SUGGESTED QUILTING LINES

STRAIGHT FOLD

DIAGONAL FOLD

1

2

2

1

PLUMERIA

Remember to add
1/8" cutting
allowance for hand
appliqué.

2

1

the Hawaiian way

PLUMERIA ©2004 Elizabeth Root · Friendship Quilts...

CENTER

STRAIGHT FOLD

7"

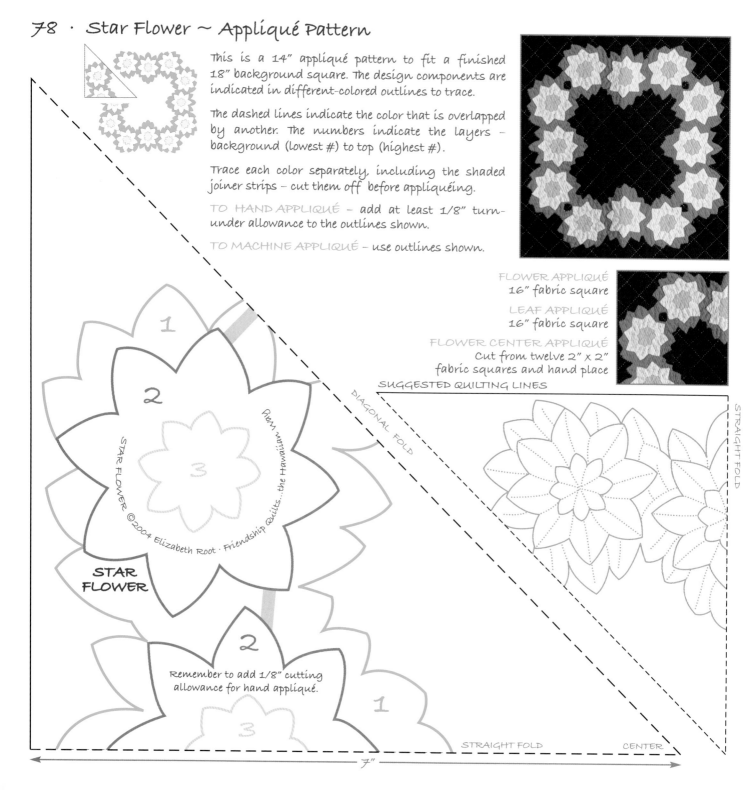

This is a 14" appliqué pattern to fit a finished 18" background square. The design components are indicated in different-colored outlines to trace.

The dashed lines indicate the color that is overlapped by another. The numbers indicate the layers – background (lowest #) to top (highest #).

Trace each color separately, including the shaded joiner strips – cut them off before appliquéing.

TO HAND APPLIQUÉ – add at least 1/8" turn-under allowance to the outlines shown.

TO MACHINE APPLIQUÉ – use outlines shown.

FLOWER APPLIQUÉ
16" fabric square

LEAF APPLIQUÉ
16" fabric square

FLOWER CENTER APPLIQUÉ
Cut from twelve 2" x 2"
fabric squares and hand place

SUGGESTED QUILTING LINES

1

2

3

STAR FLOWER ©2004 Elizabeth Root · Friendship Quilts...the Hawaiian way

STAR
FLOWER

2

Remember to add 1/8" cutting
allowance for hand appliqué.

1

3

DIAGONAL FOLD

STRAIGHT FOLD

STRAIGHT FOLD

CENTER

7"

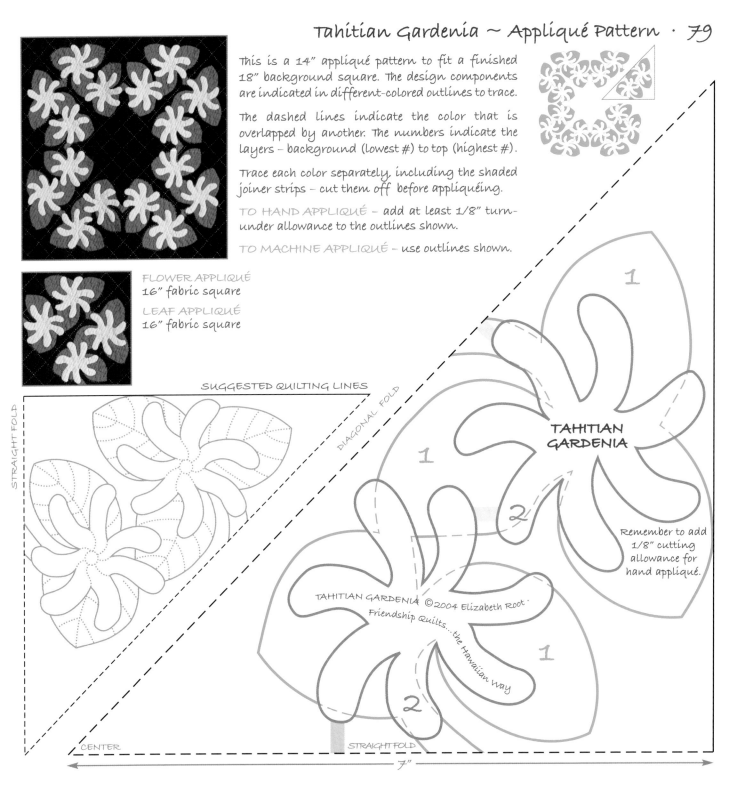

This is a 14" appliqué pattern to fit a finished 18" background square. The design components are indicated in different-colored outlines to trace.

The dashed lines indicate the color that is overlapped by another. The numbers indicate the layers – background (lowest #) to top (highest #).

Trace each color separately, including the shaded joiner strips – cut them off before appliquéing.

TO HAND APPLIQUÉ – add at least 1/8" turn-under allowance to the outlines shown.

TO MACHINE APPLIQUÉ – use outlines shown.

FLOWER APPLIQUÉ
16" fabric square

LEAF APPLIQUÉ
16" fabric square

SUGGESTED QUILTING LINES

STRAIGHT FOLD

DIAGONAL FOLD

CENTER

STRAIGHT FOLD

7"

1

1

TAHITIAN GARDENIA

2

Remember to add 1/8" cutting allowance for hand appliqué.

TAHITIAN GARDENIA ©2004 Elizabeth Root · Friendship Quilts...the Hawaiian Way

1

1

2

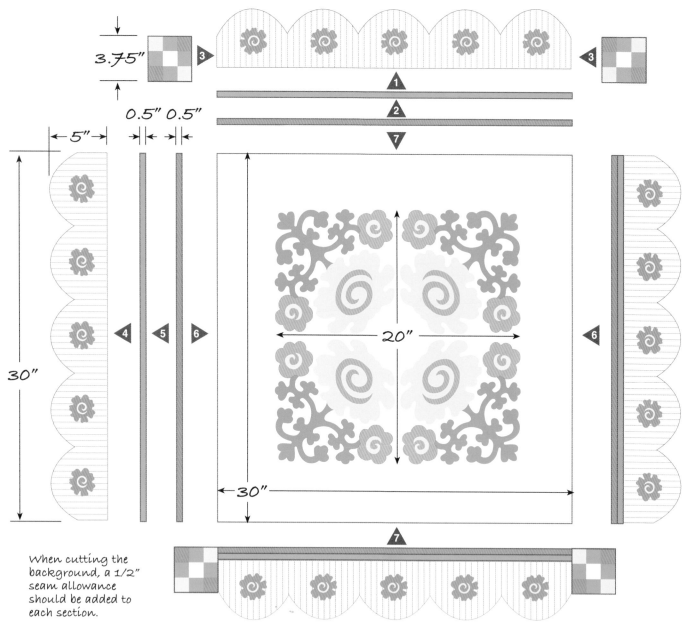

3.75"

0.5" 0.5"

5"

30"

20"

30"

When cutting the background, a 1/2" seam allowance should be added to each section.

Nine-Patch pattern
page 96

Scallop pattern
page 97

Flower pattern
page 98

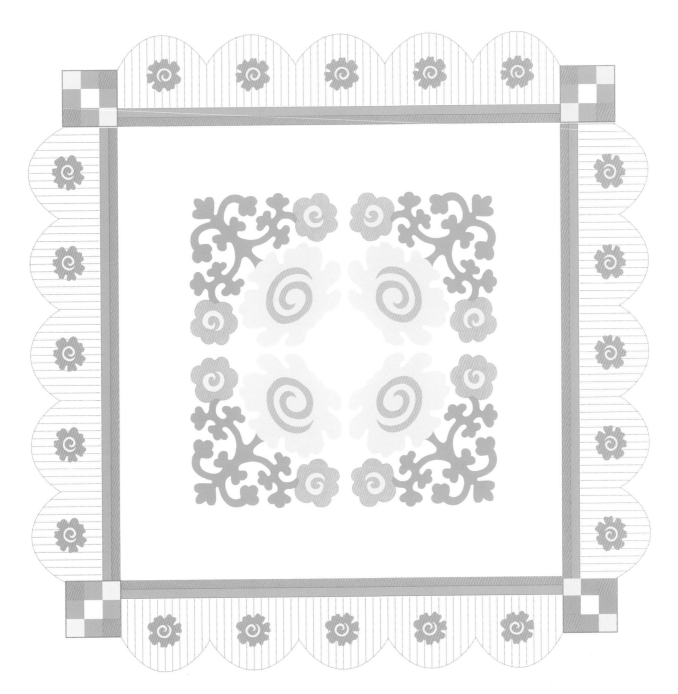

CENTER DESIGN, 82-83

This is a 20" appliqué pattern to fit a finished 30" background square. The design components are indicated in different-colored outlines to trace.

The dashed lines indicate the color that is overlapped by another. The numbers indicate the layers – background (lowest #) to top (highest #).

Trace each color separately, including the shaded joiner strips – cut them off when the appliqué has been positioned, pinned and/or basted.

HAND APPLIQUÉ – add at least 1/8" turn-under allowance to the outlines shown.

MACHINE APPLIQUÉ – use outlines shown.

FLOWER APPLIQUÉ
Large Flowers: 21" x 21"
To Hand Place: Cut 4 - 6" x 8"
Flower Center: 4" x 4"

Small Flowers: 21" x 21"
To Hand Place: Cut 8 - 3.5"x 4"
Flower Center: 2" x 2"

Flower center patterns
on page 98

LEAF APPLIQUÉ
21" x 21"

Remember to add 1/8" minimum turn-under allowance to the design outline if doing hand appliqué.

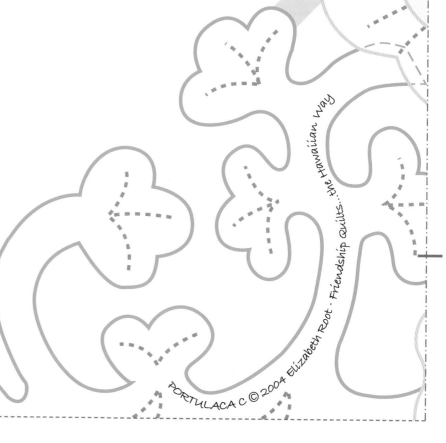

PORTULACA C © 2004 Elizabeth Root · Friendship Quilts...the Hawaiian Way

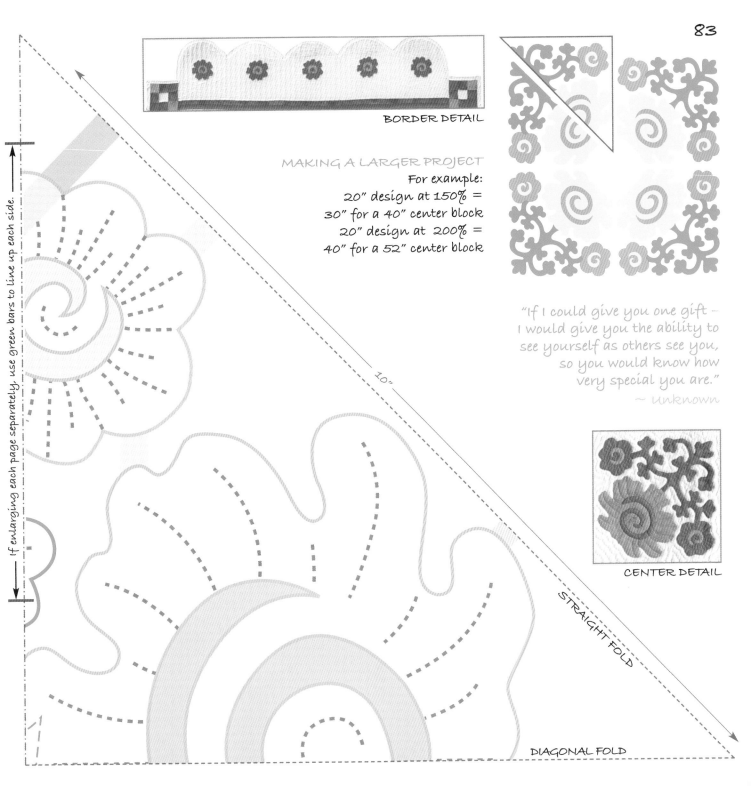

BORDER DETAIL

MAKING A LARGER PROJECT

For example:

20" design at 150% =
30" for a 40" center block
20" design at 200% =
40" for a 52" center block

"If I could give you one gift –
I would give you the ability to
see yourself as others see you,
so you would know how
very special you are."

~ Unknown

CENTER DETAIL

If enlarging each page separately, use green bars to line up each side.

10"

STRAIGHT FOLD

DIAGONAL FOLD

83

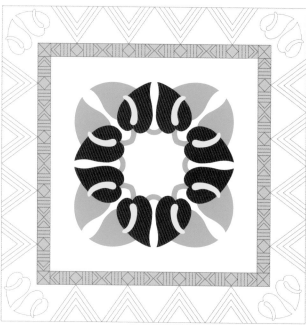

Any of the designs shown in this book can be adapted to a larger wall hanging size.
For example:
14" design at 150% = 21" for a 27" center block
14" design at 200% = 28" for a 36" center block

"Memories are stitched with love."
~ Unknown

Chevron quilting pattern
page 99

Inner border quilting
pattern – page 99 - 100

Anthurium corner
quilting pattern – page 100

When cutting the background,
a 1/2" seam allowance should
be added to each section.

Trace the individual or a group of
flowers onto the background corners
to quilt design as shown here.

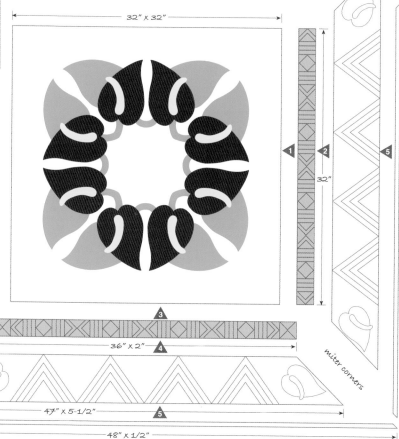

32" x 32"

32"

1 2 5

3

36" x 2"

4

miter corners

47" x 5-1/2"

5

48" x 1/2"

This is a 21" appliqué pattern (the pattern on page 42 will need to be enlarged 175% for this project) to fit a finished 32" background square. The design components are indicated in different-colored outlines to trace.

The dashed lines indicate the color that is overlapped by another. The numbers indicate the layers – background (lowest #) to top (highest #).

Trace each color separately, including the shaded joiner strips – cut them off when the appliqué has been positioned, pinned and/or basted.

HAND APPLIQUÉ – add at least 1/8" turn-under allowance to the outlines shown.

MACHINE APPLIQUÉ – use outlines shown.

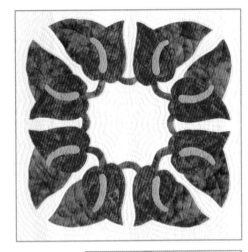

FLOWER APPLIQUÉ
Large Flowers: 22" x 22"
To Hand Place:
Cut 8 - 6.5" x 8.5"

Flower Stamens:
Cut 8 - 3" x 5.5"

LEAF APPLIQUÉ
22" X 22"

"Just thinking about a friend makes you want to do a happy dance, because a friend is someone who loves you in spite of your faults."

~ Charles M. Schulz

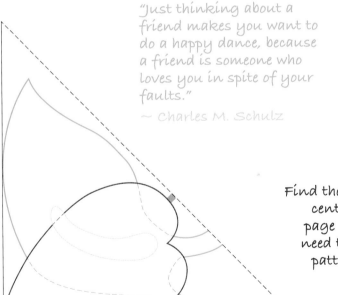

Find the Anthurium center pattern on page 42. You will need to enlarge the pattern 175% for this project.

CORNER DETAIL

INNER BORDER QUILTING DETAIL

Any of the designs shown in this book can be adapted to a larger wall hanging size.
For example:
14" design at 150% = 21" for a 27" center block
14" design at 200% = 28" for a 36" center block

*"The best kind of sleep
beneath Heaven above,
is under a quilt
handmade with love."*

~ Unknown

Chevron quilting pattern
page 99

Inner border quilting
pattern – page 99-100

Spiderlily corner
quilting pattern – page 101

When cutting the background,
a 1/2" seam allowance should
be added to each section.

Trace the individual or a group of
flowers onto the background corners
to quilt design as shown here.

32" x 32"

32"

1
2
5

3

36" x 2"

4

47" x 5-1/2"

5

48" x 1/2"

miter corners

This is a 21" appliqué pattern (the pattern on page 35 will need to be enlarged 175% for this project) to fit a finished 32" background square. The design components are indicated in different-colored outlines to trace.

The dashed lines indicate the color that is overlapped by another. The numbers indicate the layers – background (lowest #) to top (highest #).

Trace each color separately, including the shaded joiner strips – cut them off when the appliqué has been positioned, pinned and/or basted.

HAND APPLIQUÉ – add at least 1/8" turn-under allowance to the outlines shown.

MACHINE APPLIQUÉ – use outlines shown.

FLOWER APPLIQUÉ
Large Flowers: 22" x 22"
To Hand Place:
Cut eight - 6.5" x 8.5"

Flower Stamens:
Cut eight - 3" x 5.5"

LEAF APPLIQUÉ
22" X 22"

"Quilts, like friends, are different, colorful, fun, warm and comforting – you can never acquire enough of either."
~ Unknown

Find the Spiderlily center pattern on page 35. You will need to enlarge the pattern 175% for this project.

BORDER QUILTING DETAIL

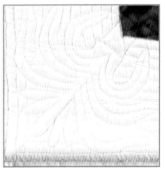

CORNER DETAIL

CORNER A
8" X 8"
Appliqué Pattern, page 90

VINE END B
5.75" X 6.25"
Appliqué Pattern, page 91

VINE CENTER C
7.5" X 7.5"
Appliqué Pattern, page 92

VINE CENTER D
7.5" X 7.5"
Appliqué Pattern, page 93

Cutting the Vine Borders

The vine portion of the borders in this book is made of 2 center patterns and an end pattern. They can be made any length in increments of 7.5" (center patterns C and D) plus the 5.75" end (B).

Fabric Allowances for Border Corner

Vine (4): cut each quarter separately from four 7.5 x 6" squares, folded diagonally
Flower, large (4): cut from four 6.5" x 5.5" squares, folded in half
Flowers, small (8): cut from eight 3" x 3" squares
Flower centers: large (4): cut from four 4" x 3" squares
small (8): cut from eight 1.5" x 1.5" squares

Fabric Allowances for the Vine Borders

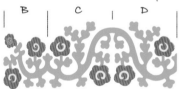

Used in Name Quilt, page 64

Border using 1 end and 2 center section patterns
(2 ends + 4 center sections)
One color border: 41.5" x 7.5", cut four - 45" x 9"
Multi-color border (vine): 41.5" x 7.5", cut four - 45" x 9"
Flowers (hand placed), large: cut 188 - 3" x 3"; small: cut 8 - 2" x 2"
Flower centers, large: cut 188 - 1.5" x 1.5"; small, cut 8 - 1" x 1"

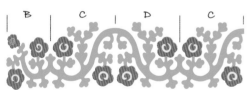

Used in Lei Quilt, page 40
and Portulaca Quilt, page 51

Border using 1 end and 3 center section patterns
(2 ends + 6 center sections)
One color border: 56.5" x 7.5", cut four - 60" x 9"
Multi-color border (vine): 45.5" x 7.5", cut four - 50" x 9"
Flowers (hand placed), large: cut 188 - 3" x 3"; small: cut 8 - 2" x 2"
Flower centers, large: cut 188 - 1.5" x 1.5"; small, cut 8 - 1" x 1"

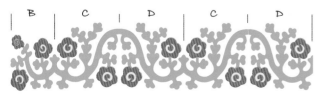

Used in Garden Quilt, page 24

Border using 1 end and 4 center section patterns
(2 ends + 8 center sections)
One color border: 71.5" x 7.5", cut four - 75" x 9"
Multi-color border (vine): 71.5" x 7.5", cut four - 75" x 9"
Flowers (hand placed), large: cut 188 - 3" x 3"; small: cut 8 - 2" x 2"
Flower centers, large: cut 188 - 1.5" x 1.5"; small, cut 8 - 1" x 1"

Making Your Vine Border Pattern

Cut a piece of tracing paper the length of the border of the chosen quilt design. Draw a straight line along the bottom of the paper to keep the pattern sections in position as you trace them. To find the center point, fold the length of paper in half. Unfold paper and starting from the center to the right, mark off the number of segments you will need, including the end section. Trace the sections for one half of the design (D). Fold the length of the tracing paper in half and line up the straight lines. Trace the other half of the border design (E). Cut the pattern out (F).

Diagram D - Mark sections, trace pattern on one half.

Fold paper, trace other half. - **Diagram E**

Diagram F - Cut out pattern.

Trace pattern on appliqué fabric. - **Diagram G**

Cutting Your Vine Border ~ One Color

Secure the border pattern to the appliqué fabric and trace (G). The turn-under allowance will be added later during cutting. Place and center the appliqué fabric on the background section which has its seam allowances included in its measurement. Pin and baste securely, making sure that it is straight along the background edge (H). Following the outline of the appliqué pattern, add a minimum of 1/8" turn-under allowance, and then either cut away the excess fabric <u>before</u> you begin to appliqué, or cut away the excess fabric <u>as</u> you appliqué (I).

Diagram H - Cut out appliqué (adding 1/8" turn-under beyond traced line), baste to background fabric, then appliqué.

OR

Baste appliqué fabric with pattern line drawn onto - **Diagram I** background fabric. Cut away excess design fabric as you appliqué.

Cutting Your Vine Border ~ Multi-Color

Cut out entire border pattern as if making a one-color design – follow directions above (H/I). But, before appliquéing, position colored flowers, shown in pink in diagram (K), over those in the green vine pattern. Carefully pin in place on the background only. Cut off green-colored flowers underneath, leaving enough of the stem to slip under the pink flowers. Be sure to leave enough allowance so that the appliquéd flowers cover the stem.

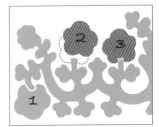

Diagram J
(1) Cut away green flower, as shown; (2) replace flower with selected color; (3) appliqué flower over green stem.

Flower Centers

For directions, see page 100. Enlarge or reduce the spiral center pattern on that page as necessary. For one-color designs, either add a second color, or use the reverse appliqué method where the background color becomes the center color.

Cut design out the pattern on the eighth fold. Cut the spiral centers for the flowers separately and hand place before appliquéing.

CENTER

DIAGONAL FOLD

STRAIGHT FOLD

8"

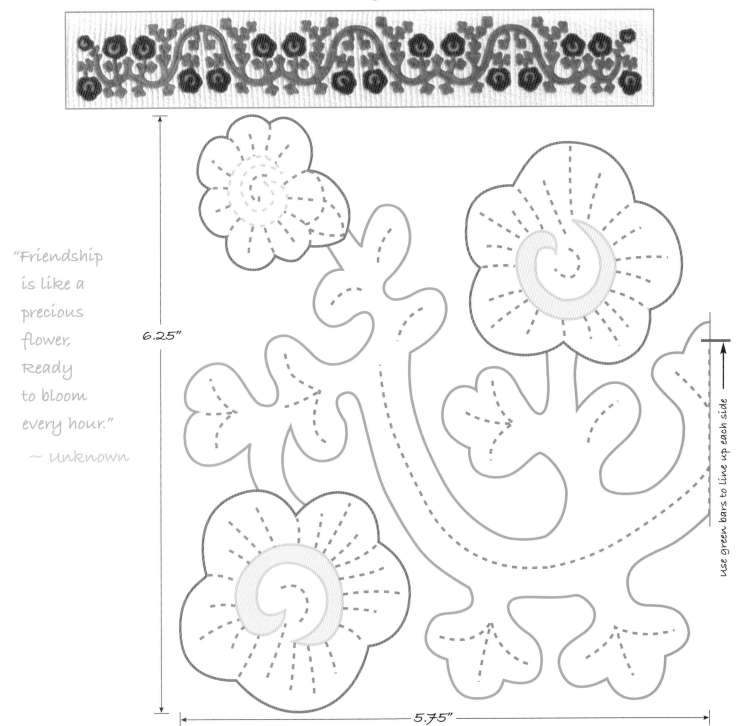

"Friendship
is like a
precious
flower,
Ready
to bloom
every hour."

~ Unknown

6.25"

5.75"

use green bars to line up each side

use green bars to line up each side

7.5"

7.5"

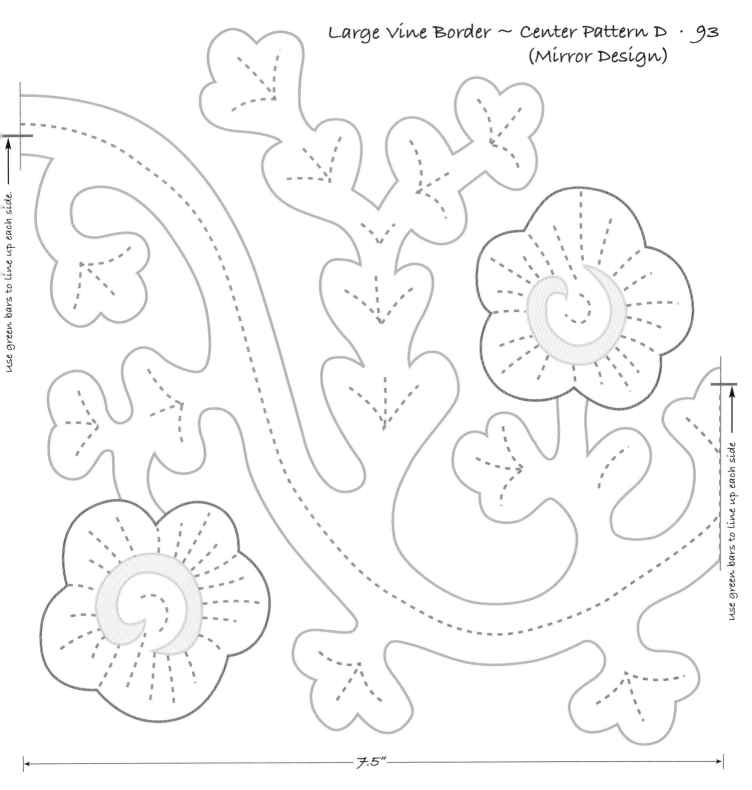

Large Vine Border ~ Center Pattern D · 93
(Mirror Design)

use green bars to line up each side.

use green bars to line up each side

7.5"

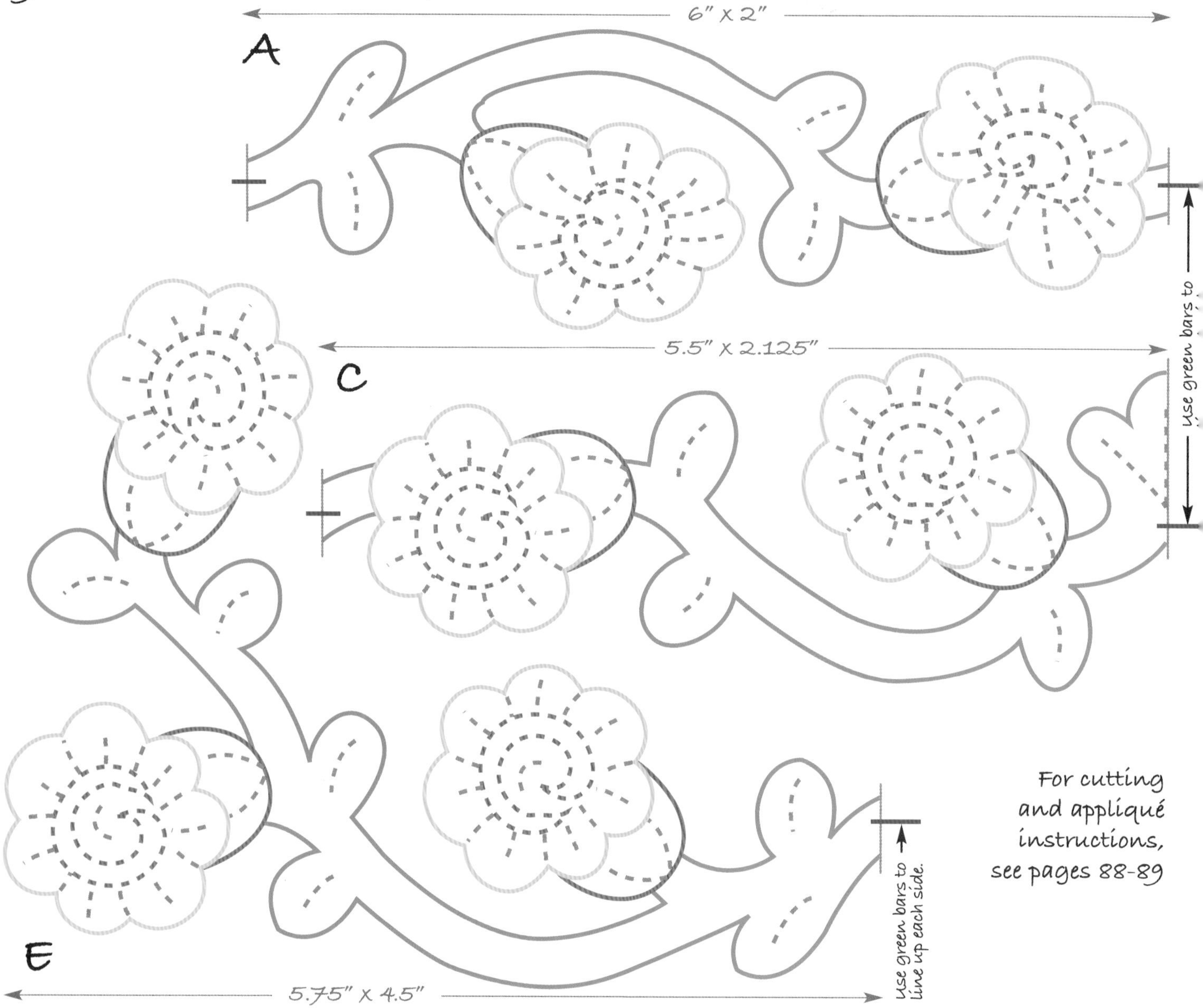

A

6" x 2"

C

5.5" x 2.125"

use green bars to

E

5.75" x 4.5"

use green bars to line up each side.

For cutting and appliqué instructions, see pages 88-89

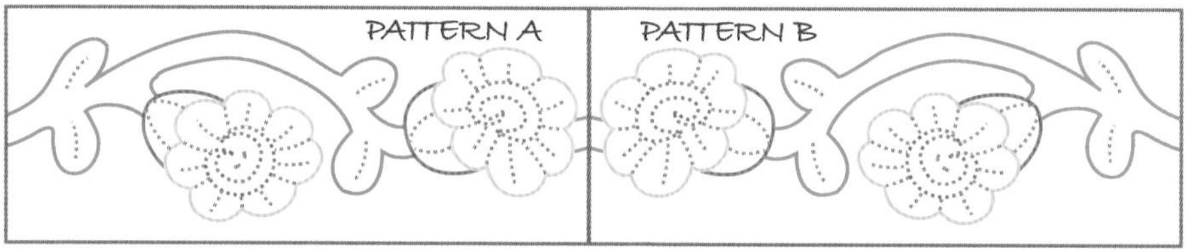

PATTERN A   PATTERN B

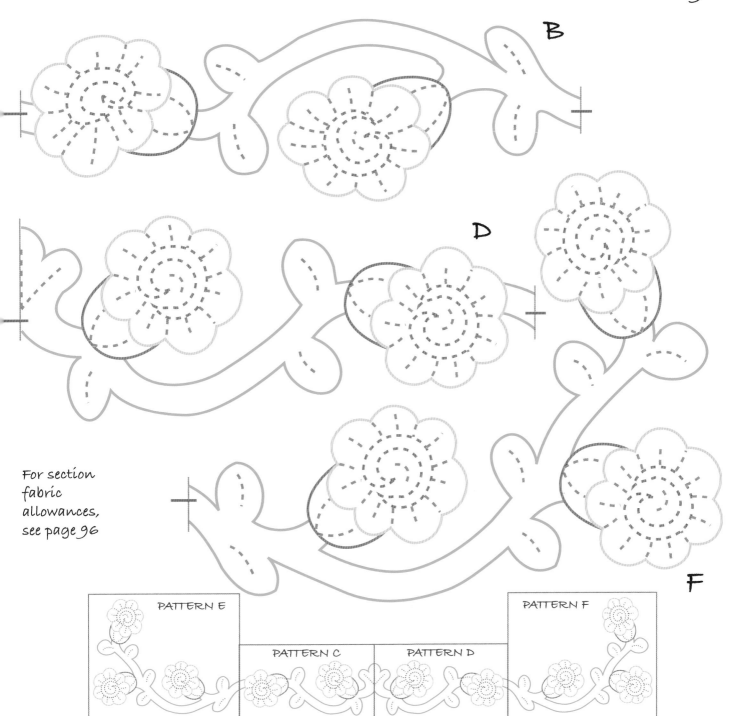

B

D

For section
fabric
allowances,
see page 96

F

PATTERN E

PATTERN F

PATTERN C

PATTERN D

Fabric Allowances for the Small Vine Borders

The inner border vine patterns are made up of sections that can be mixed and matched to create any length border desired. The two center sections can be used individually or combined together, or also combined with the end section. Choose the desired border configuration and then add up the fabric for each section. When appliquéing multi-color borders, you may want to also cut the flowers from one length of fabric rather than cutting and placing individually. You would then cut away the excess fabric after basting the line of flowers in place.

End Border Section
One color border: 5.75" x 4.5"; Second color flowers: 5.75" x 4.5";
Flowers (hand placed), three per section each 1.75" x 1.5", Cut three - 2.5" x 2"

Center Border Section
One color border: 5.5" x 2.125"; Second color flowers: 5.5" x 2.125";
Flowers (hand placed), three per section each 1.75" x 1.5", Cut three - 2.5" x 2"

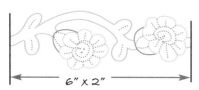

Center Border Section
One color border: 6" x 2"; Second color flowers: 6" x 2";
Flowers (hand placed), three per section each 1.75" x 1.5", Cut three - 2.5" x 2"

Nine-Patch Blocks

The Friendship Lei Quilt (p. 40; 16 blocks), the White Flower Wall Quilt (p. 74; 4 blocks) and the Portulaca Wall quilt (p. 51; 4 blocks) include the 3.75" nine-patch block. Below is the pattern and diagram of how to construct the patchwork block.

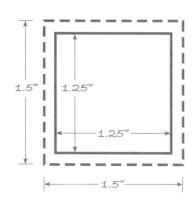

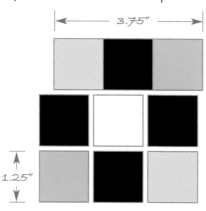

Sew three sets of 3 color squares together into horizontal rows. Then sew three rows together vertically to make the nine-patch squares

From White Flower Quilt p. 74

From Lei Quilt p. 40

From Portulaca Wall Quilt p. 80

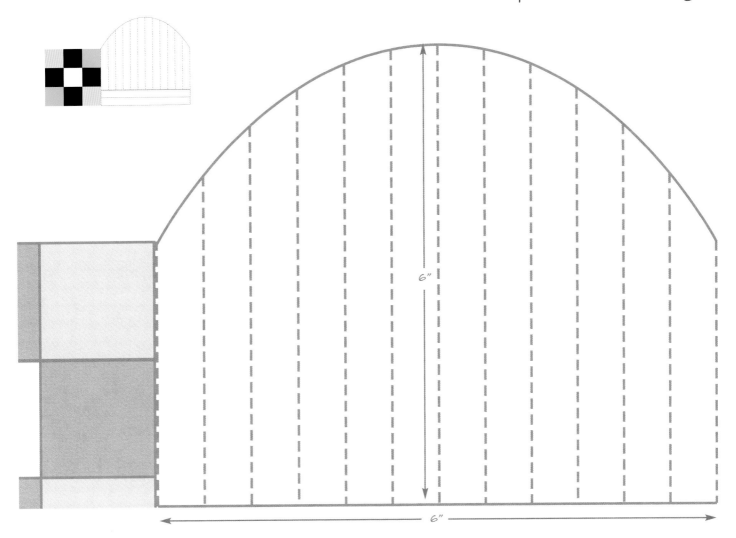

Determining Size and How Many Scallops You'll Need

Determine the length of the border. Choose the desired number of scallops. Divide the border length by that number; this will give you each scallop size. Adjust measurement to the nearest 1/4", 1/2", or to the nearest inch. This will also adjust and determine the finished the size of your project. Or, you can determine your scallop size first and design your project accordingly.

...continued on page 108

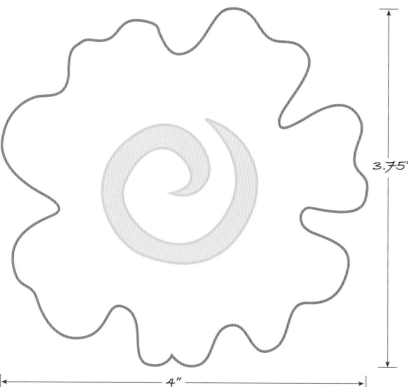

3.75"

4"

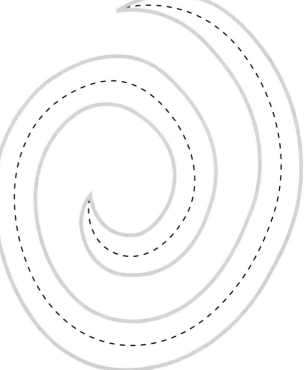

2.25"

2.375"

INDIVIDUAL FLOWER PATTERNS USED IN QUILT PROJECTS ON PAGES 68, 72, 74, AND 80.

 The spiral centers in the larger Portulaca quilt projects on pages 38, 70, and 82 are not symmetrical. They should be cut and appliquéd separately. The rest of the design is cut on the eighth.

Trace the spiral patterns. Add at least 1/8" turn-under allowance. Position on the petal and appliqué. This will give the center of your flowers a three-dimensional look.

Alternately, you can reverse appliqué the centers. Trace the dashed line on the patterns to the right onto the petal fabric. Cut along the line. Place the center color fabric underneath the petal fabric. Make sure that it is positioned so that when you turn back the edges of the spiral design, the center color shows. Baste in place. Appliqué the turned edges of the petal fabric. Make sure your stitches go through to the background fabric.

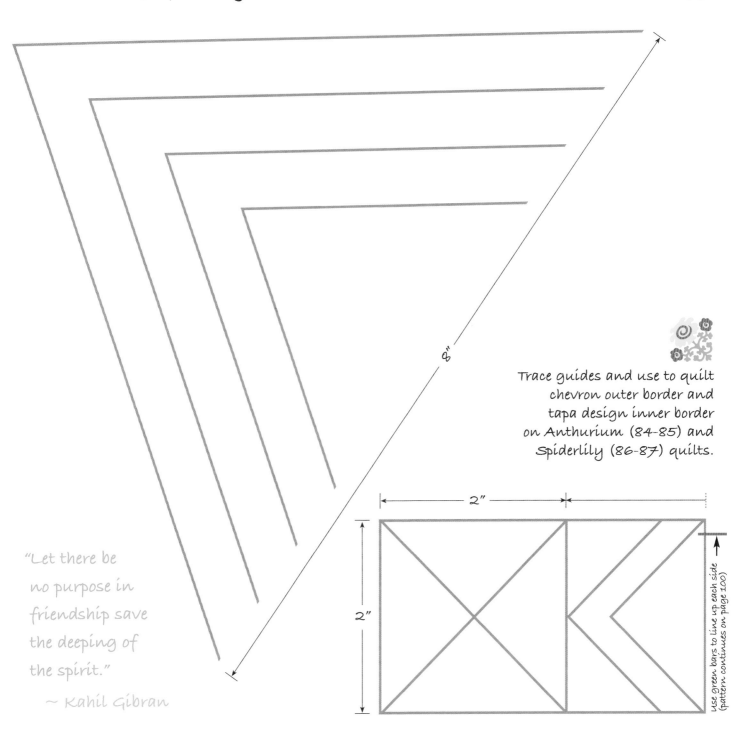

8"

2"

2"

Trace guides and use to quilt chevron outer border and tapa design inner border on Anthurium (84-85) and Spiderlily (86-87) quilts.

use green bars to line up each side (pattern continues on page 100)

"Let there be no purpose in friendship save the deeping of the spirit."

~ Kahil Gibran

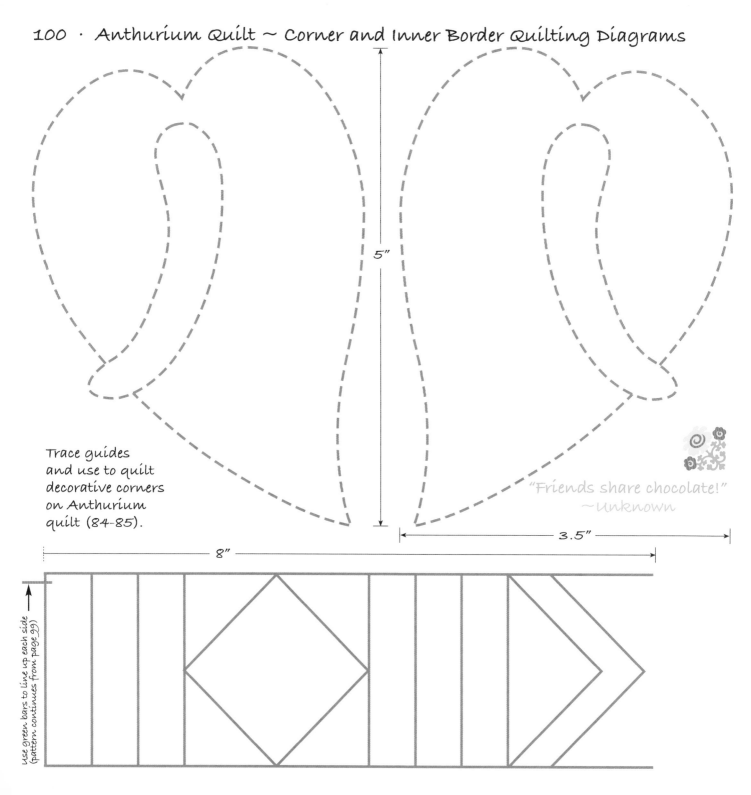

Trace guides
and use to quilt
decorative corners
on Anthurium
quilt (84-85).

5"

3.5"

8"

"Friends share chocolate!"
~ Unknown

use green bars to line up each side
(pattern continues from page 99)

" 'Tis the privilege of friendship to
talk nonsense, and have that
nonsense respected."
    ~ Charles Lamb (1775 - 1834)

Trace guides
and use to quilt
decorative corners
on Anthurium
quilt (84-85).

9"

6.25"

DETERMINING HOW MUCH FABRIC YOU'LL NEED

Measure the eighth pattern from the center point along the straight to the edge of the appliqué pattern. Double that measurement and add an inch cutting allowance all around. The fabric square will be that measurement vertically and horizontally. For example, for a 7" measurement, double to 14". Add one inch minimum for a 16" x 16" square – to allow a little leeway.

If hand-placing design components, measure and add at least 1/2" all around and cut the number of pieces required.

7"

TOTAL PATTERN on fabric folded into eighths

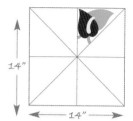

14"

14"

WORKING WITH MULTICOLOR DESIGNS

Most of the patterns in this book should be constructed as multicolor designs. You will see in the preceding patterns, the flower (and flower parts) and leaves have the cutting line designated in a different color. When working with two or more color appliqué, measure each color. Be sure to cut each pattern piece (leaves, flowers, etc.) from the folded fabric (eighth fold) for easiest placement. Position the pieces in the same place as shown on the pattern. Save any excess fabric for future projects.

If you want to make the stamens a different color, cut out individually and hand place.

FLOWER PATTERN PLACEMENT

+

LEAF PATTERN PLACEMENT

+

STAMEN PATTERN PLACEMENT

=

Remember, the solid line shown is the cutting line for fusible fabric techniques. If you are hand appliquéing, add your desired turn-under allowance before tracing and cutting out the paper pattern. Don't forget to include any joiner strips and/or any extra fabric indicated for layering the design.

USING JOINER STRIPS

Some pattern parts have joiner strips indicated. This is so you can cut the design out on the eighth fabric fold, all at once, to ensure exact alignment with other parts of the design. The joiner strips will be cut off after the appliqué fabric has been pinned or basted to the background. You can alternately cut the flower portions separately and hand place them, but this method is not always as exact.

"Quilt 'til you wilt!" ~ Unknown

Quilting
Instructions

 Just Some Suggestions

 REMEMBER you can always cut off the excess fabric, but using too little fabric cannot be reversed. Always preshrink your fabric, if necessary. If using fusible techniques, wash and iron your fabric as coatings may hinder the fusible web from adhering to the fabric.

 Choosing your fabrics. Buy the best quality materials you can afford. You will be investing a lot of time and effort in the making of your Hawaiian-style quilt masterpiece, especially if hand appliquéing and quilting. By the time you're finished, you'll want it to last a lifetime...maybe longer.

 Choosing your colors. Traditionally, highly contrasting solid colors are used. There is no right or wrong color combination. Use your favorite colors or whatever blends best with your decor. Color can be bold and highly contrasting; subtle and pastel; two of the same color family, one light and one dark, or multiple colors. Fabrics can be solids, prints, textures, cotton, chintz, silk, whatever strikes your fancy. There is no right or wrong choice. The hand-painted or batik fabrics available offer wonderful variations.

 The batting (and muslin, if making a pillow) should be a larger square than the background fabric. How much depends on the weight of the batting. Thicker batting will shrink the finished size more when quilted than a thinner batting. Add a minimum two extra inches all around for a pillow-size project and up to four extra inches all around for a wall hanging-size project.

 Choosing your quilting style. Traditionally, echo style is used. But you can also use any quilting design that you like or that better suits the look of the finished piece. Many times very lacy, delicate, busy, appliqué patterns look better with a cross hatch (small squares) behind them to accentuate the design. Early Hawaiian quilts used a variety of quilting patterns. If you are a sewing machine whiz, try machine appliqué and quilting if using fusible fabric techniques.

 Always quilt right against the edge of the appliquéd design when hand quilting. This makes the design appear a little raised above the background fabric.

 Your mood will be reflected in your stitching. Calm and happy or angry and annoyed – your mood will show in your stitching. A little calm quilting each day and you will finish in no time. Above all, enjoy what you're doing. Despite how anxious you are to see the finished piece, don't rush your work. From start to finish, time taken to ensure each step is properly done will save you time and disappointment later on.

CUTTING, PINNING AND BASTING: With these first steps, it is very important to be as precise as possible as they are the foundation of your finished work. Cutting without letting the layers slip, smoothing the design gently from the center outward so it is flat against the background before pinning and basting, ensures problem-free appliquéing and quilting later on.

APPLIQUÉ: Appliqué using a single thread about 18" long to prevent tangling. Use the same color thread as the design color to help hide the stitches. Strive for no less than 8 appliqué stitches per inch. It's okay to snip the fabric to help you turn it under more easily. But always take a few extra stitches to prevent the fabric from fraying. Take an extra stitch at the tip of a point.

QUILTING: Start with no fewer than eight stitches per inch; that's four on the front and four on the back. As you gain more control over your needle, set your goal at 16 to 20 stitches per inch. It is more important to make your stitches and spaces even than to make tiny stitches with large spaces. Quilt rows should be a consistent width – 1/2" to 3/4" wide or as small as 1/4" for miniatures.

"My soul is fed…by my needle and thread." ~ Unknown

Cutting, pinning and basting

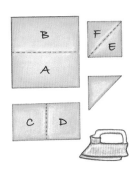

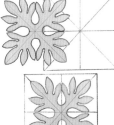
overlap allowance

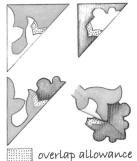

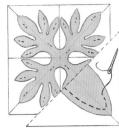
enlarged

Prewash, iron, cut, fold appliqué/background fabric, right sides up, as shown.
1. Fold A up to B.
2. Fold C over to D.
3. Fold E up to F.
4. Iron in folds on both fabrics.

Place pattern on fabric, as shown. Pin through all layers OR trace around pattern with a pencil, then pin. Cut out design.

If making a multi-colored design: follow the pattern and cut each color separately. Add enough fabric to allow for overlapping elements, e.g. flower under or stem; basket over stem.

Open folded, cut appliqué/background fabrics, right sides up. Ease appliqué folds to match background folds and your design is automatically centered.

Pin design to background, without stretching fabric. Keep folds lined up as possible. Baste 1/4" inside edge of appliqué. Keep fabrics smooth, and wrinkle free. Remove pins.

Appliqué

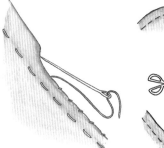 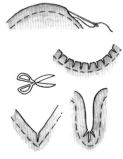 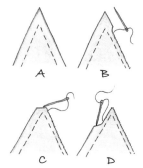  

Patterns allow for an average 1/8" turn-under. Use the 1/4" basting line as a guide and turn fabric under until it hits basting stitches. Use the tip of your needle to help turn under the fabric ahead as you appliqué.

Ease fabric under, without stretching it, for outside curves. Inside curves and valleys: snip as needed to help ease fabric under neatly. Always take extra stitches at the snips to prevent fraying.

A) Points, as in the tips of leaves. B) Appliqué up one side to 2 or 3 stitches from point. C) Turn point under, cut away excess fabric if needed, but always try to allow 1/8" turn under. D) Fold under remaining side and appliqué.

Cutouts and slits. Mark desired appliqué line around cutout or slit and appliqué using inside curve and valley methods. You may opt not to make cutouts and slits in a design.

Appliqué the entire design. Take out basting stitches. Look over your appliqué work and see if it needs to be cleaned. If so, wash in warm water with ivory flakes. Gently iron.

Quilting

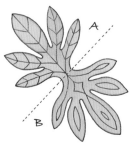   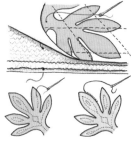 

Follow the suggested quilting lines on the pattern selected or design your own quilting lines. Make the appliqué quilting: A) realistic, or B) echo style. Background quilting is traditionally echo style.

For a wall hanging, layer appliqué on batting, batting on backing fabric. For a pillow, use muslin as backing. Save backing fabric for pillow back. Cut batting at least 2" larger all around than fabric squares.

Pin layers together, smooth fabric from center as you pin toward the edge. Baste layers together in a grid pattern. Keep smoothing layers, pin as necessary. When finished, remove pins.

With the first stitch, catch the knot of a single thread in the batting. First quilt the appliquéd design. The first row of quilting on the background goes right against the appliquéd edge. Quilt around the appliqué.

Continue to quilt toward the edges. When quilted, remove basting stitches. Trim batting. You are ready to finish the quilt block as a pillow, wall hanging, or any way you wish.

Finishing

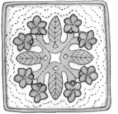 

PILLOWS

The simplest way of finishing a pillow is to put the right sides of the quilted square and the backing fabric together. Sew around three sides and four corners, leaving enough room to add your pillow form. Hand stitch the opening closed.

You can also add cording

and a zipper to the back

Other things to do with your Hawaiian-style quilt masterpieces...

Euro Pillow for your bed...Futons for the floor...Add multiple borders for larger wall hangings... Put multiple blocks of the same or different designs together for even larger wall hangings or a long wall hanging above a couch or bed...Put two blocks together with shoulder straps for a great quilter's tote to hold your work in progress.

WALL HANGINGS

Adding a sleeve

Cut a width of fabric the same size as your finished wall hanging. It is best to use the same color. Seam the edges with a one-inch allowance on both sides. With right sides together, hand sew the top of the strip to the top of the quilt. Then fold fabric down and sew the bottom to the back of the quilt. This will make a sleeve to hold a rod to hang your quilt.

Adding tabs

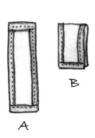

A

B

Measure the width of the wall hanging. Determine how many hanging tabs are needed. For three inches showing above your wall hanging, cut out 10" x 3" strips. Sew a 1/2-inch turn seam all around (A). Fold in half. (B), right sides out, hand sew tabs an equal distance apart, through both layers. Thread the rod through tabs to hang.

Marking and Drawing Scallop Design On Your Border Fabric

Using the template, trace the scallop outline from both ends toward the center, so if any adjustment is needed, you can make it in the center of the section (Diagram A).

Do not cut out on the drawn line. After the entire quilt have been quilted, including the borders, hand baste along the scallop cut line to keep layers from shifting, then cut out along the marked scallop line (B).

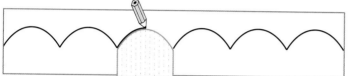

Diagram A - Trace from both ends; adjust middle scallop(s) if necessary.

Diagram B - After border is quilted, baste marked scallop line and then cut out.

Making and Attaching Your Bias Strip

A bias binding is a must for binding curved edges. Cut your binding strips at a 45 degree angle, and join with diagonal seams pressed open. Or, you can use a suitable bias tape. A single binding cut at 1-1/4" will finish to 1/4". Press the edge that will lay on your quilt top, under 1/4". (C).

With right sides together and the raw edge of the binding aligned with the marked border, begin stitching a 1/4" seam at the top of the scallop. You can do this by hand or by machine. Stitch to the base of the "V" (D).

If sewing by machine, stop with the needle down at that point. Lift the presser foot, pivot the quilt and binding to begin sewing out of the V. Put the presser foot down and sew out of the "V", taking care not to stitch any pleats in the binding. Continue around the quilt in this manner, easing the binding around the curves, not stretching it. Overlap the beginning edge by 1", trim off at an angle.

Diagram C
Cut binding strips on the diagonal (bias). Piece together to make one strip. Or, use bias tape.

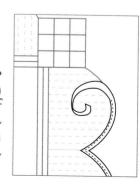

Diagram D
Sew binding onto front of quilt first, turn and finish binding on back.

It is common practice for each person making a quilt block to embroider their name in the center or at the bottom corner of the finished square after the entire quilt has been quilted. A short saying or sentiment can also be embroidered, space allowing. Embroidery is most easily done using Perle Cotton, using all strands in an appropriate size. The colors used for each block can vary or be all the same.

Below are a couple of basic embroidery stitches that are commonly used - there are hundreds more decorative stitches that you can find in myriad embroidery books or on the internet.

You will find a few friendship sayings throughout this book that may inspire you to add them or to create special ones of your own. You should also include the date the project is finished on the quilt.

Backstitch

This stitch is used for lines and outlines. Backstitch is done from right to left. Bring the thread up on the line (1) and insert needle a little to the right (2). Now bring needle up again an equal distance ahead (3). Insert again at beginning of the last stitch (4).

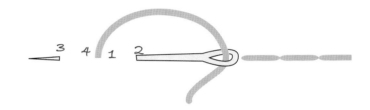

"Quilting with a friend will keep you in stitches." ~ Unknown

French Knot

This stitch is used for dots. To work a French knot, bring the thread out at the required position (1), hold the thread with the thumb and wrap the thread twice round the needle (2). Hold the twists on the needle with the index finger and re-insert the needle close to where it came out (3). When the needle is halfway through the fabric, stop and arrange the knot neatly but not too tightly on the surface of the fabric. Gently pull the needle and thread though (4).

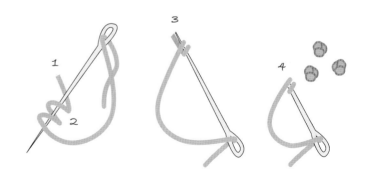

If the knot disappears, you may have twisted the thread the wrong way round the needle. Varying the number of times the thread is wrapped round the needle point will vary the size of the knot but 2 or 3 wraps is most common.

Let Friendship Bloom

A B C D E F G

H I J K L M N

O P Q R S T

U V W X Y Z

abcdefghij

klmnopqr

stuvwxyz

123456

7890

The
Cross Stitch
Designs
and Charts

Bird of Paradise XS Chart

STITCH COUNT:

Total: 95 x 95
1/4 chart: 47.5 x 47.5
Center horizontal and vertical lines share a center stitch, as shown by arrows

* When rotating this chart, work center rows (shown by black arrows) only once.

FINISHED SIZES (approximate):

18 count: 5.5" x 5.5"
14 count: 6.75" x 6.75"
11 count: 8.75" x 8.75"

TO BACK STITCH IN COLOR

Blue Anther
(3 strands):
Blue Violet DK
DMC 3746
A/B 1030

Petals and center design:
Burnt Orange
DMC 947
A/B 330

Pod and leaves:
Hunter Green VYDK
DMC 895
A/B 1044

work these rows only once as you work each quadrant of the design

X	DMC	A/B	Color	X	DMC	A/B	Color
√	744	301	Yellow-Pale	⊠	3802	1019	Antique Mauve-VY DK
m	742	303	Tangerine-LT	♣	3041	871	Antique Violet-MD
♣	740	316	Tangerine	a	368	214	Pistachio Green-LT
—	310	403	Black	◣	367	217	Pistachio Green-DK

"Take time to love the little things."
~ Unknown

116

Blue Jade
XS Chart

STITCH COUNT:

Total: 111 x 111
1/4 chart: 55.5 x 55.5
Center horizontal and
vertical lines share a
center stitch, as
shown by arrows

* When rotating
this chart, work
center rows (shown
by black arrows)
only once.

FINISHED SIZES
(approximate):

18 count: 6.25" x 6.25"
14 count: 8" x 8"
11 count: 10" x 10"

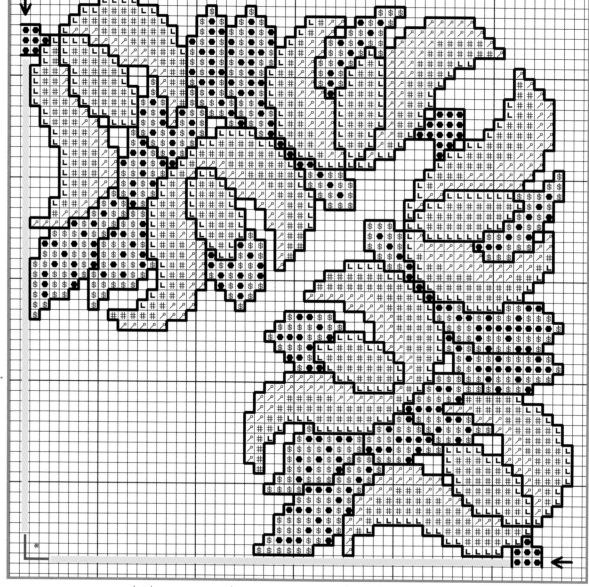

work these rows only once as you work each quadrant of the design

TO BACK STITCH
IN COLOR

Flowers:
Teal Green DK
DMC 3847
A/B 1076
───────
Leaves:
Hunter Green VY DK
DMC 895
A/B 1044

X	DMC	A/B	Color	X	DMC	A/B	Color
●	904	258	Parrot Green-VY DK	L	3847	1068	Teal Green-DK
$	906	256	Parrot Green-MD	#	3849	1064	Teal Green-LT
♪	3811	928	Turquoise-VY LT	—	310	403	Black

"Strangers are just friends waiting to happen."
~ Unknown

118

Orchid XS Chart

STITCH COUNT:

Total: 103 x 103
1/4 chart: 51.5 x 51.5
Center horizontal and
vertical lines share a
center stitch, as
shown by arrows

* When rotating
this chart, work
center rows (shown
by black arrows)
only once.

FINISHED SIZES
(approximate):

18 count: 5.75" x 5.75"
14 count: 7.5" x 7.5"
11 count: 9.5" x 9.5"

TO BACK STITCH
IN COLOR

Flowers:
Shell Gray DK
DMC 451
A/B 233

Yellow Center:
Topaz DK
DMC 782
A/B 307

Green Lip:
Moss Green
DMC 581
A/B 280

Leaves:
Pistachio Green VY DK
DMC 319
A/B 218

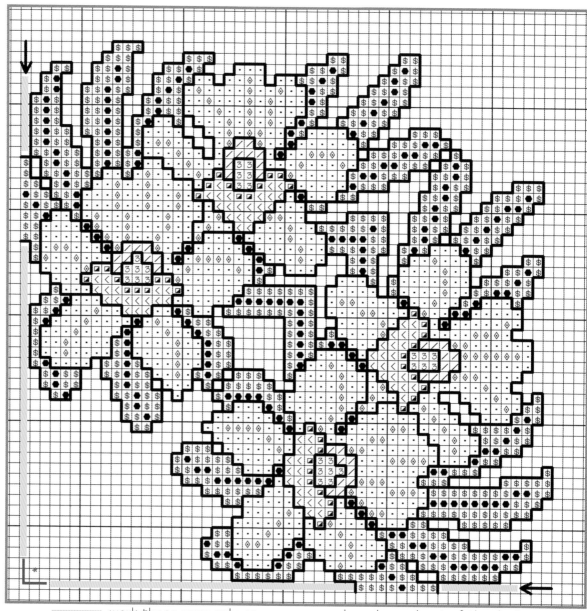

work these rows only once as you work each quadrant of the design

X	DMC	A/B	Color	X	DMC	A/B	Color
◊	3743	869	Antique Violet-VY LT	◪	581	280	Moss Green
╱	726	295	Topaz-LT	●	904	258	Parrot Green-VY DK
3	972	298	Canary-DK	$	906	256	Parrot Green-MD
<	166	279	Moss Green-MD LT	·	White	2	White
—	310	403	Black				

"Side by side or miles apart, dear friends are always close to the heart."
~ Unknown

120

Passion Flower XS Chart

STITCH COUNT:

Total: 109 x 109
1/4 chart: 54.5 x 54.5
Center horizontal and
vertical lines share a
center stitch, as
shown by arrows

* When rotating
this chart, work
center rows (shown
by black arrows)
only once.

FINISHED SIZES
(approximate):

18 count: 6" x 6"
14 count: 8" x 8"
11 count: 10" x 10"

TO BACK STITCH
IN COLOR

Flowers:
Medium Violet
DMC 552
A/B 99

Leaves:
Hunter Green VY DK
DMC 895
A/B 1044

Center:
Golden Olive DK
DMC 830
A/B 277

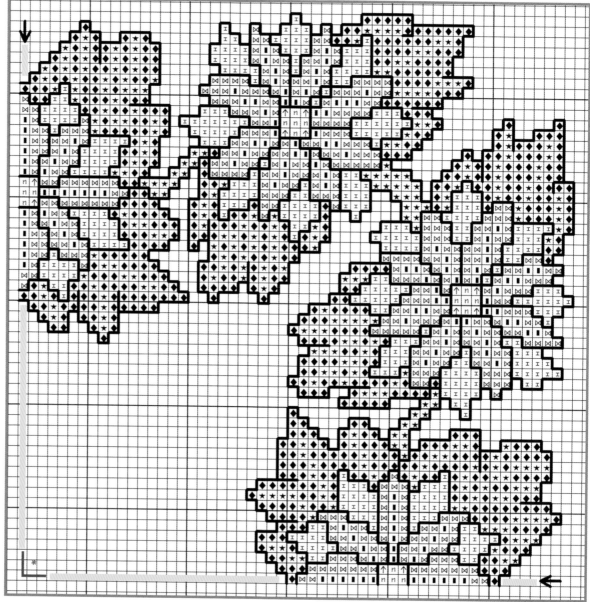

work these rows only once as you work each quadrant of the design

X	DMC	A/B	Color	X	DMC	A/B	Color
⋈	153	95	Violet-VY LT	★	3345	268	Hunter Green-DK
↑	165	253	Moss Green-VY LT	◆	3346	267	Hunter Green
▮	553	98	Violet	ɪ	3747	120	Blue Violet-VY LT
—	310	403	Black	n	832	907	Golden Olive

"Wishing to be friends is quick work, but friendship is a slow-ripening fruit."
~ Aristotle (4th Century B.C.)

Pink Ginger XS Chart

STITCH COUNT:

Total: 93 x 93
1/4 chart: 46.5 x 46.5
Center horizontal and vertical lines share a center stitch, as shown by arrows

* When rotating this chart, work center rows (shown by black arrows) only once.

FINISHED SIZES (approximate):

18 count: 5.25" x 5.25"
14 count: 6.75" x 6.75"
11 count: 8.5" x 8.5"

TO BACK STITCH IN COLOR

Flowers:
Cranberry VY DK
DMC 600
A/B 59

Leaves:
Hunter Green DVY DK
DMC 895
A/B 1044

Center:
Blue Green VY DK
DMC 500
A/B 683

work these rows only once as you work each quadrant of the design

X	DMC	A/B	Color		X	DMC	A/B	Color
·	White	2	White		✎	501	878	Blue Green-DK
‖	605	50	Cranberry-VY LT		«	503	876	Blue Green-MD
⊙	603	62	Cranberry		¢	470	267	Avocado Green-LT
♥	601	57	Cranberry-DK		⊙	469	267	Avocado Green
—	310	403	Black					

"A friend hears the song in my heart and sings it to me when my memory fails."
~ Unknown

Plumeria XS Chart

STITCH COUNT:

Total: 109 x 109
1/4 chart: 54.5 x 54.5
Center horizontal and
vertical lines share a
center stitch, as
shown by arrows

* When rotating
this chart, work
center rows (shown
by black arrows)
only once.

FINISHED SIZES
(approximate):

18 count: 6" x 6"
14 count: 8" x 8"
11 count: 10" x 10"

TO BACK STITCH
IN COLOR

Flowers:
Medium Dusty Rose
DMC 962
A/B 75
_____

Leaves:
Hunter Green DK
DMC 3345
A/B 268
_____

Small Connecting
Branch:
Golden Olive
DMC 832
A/B 907

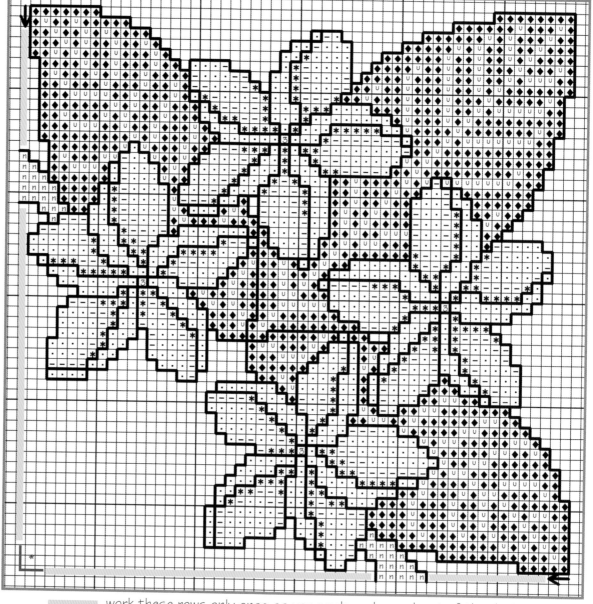

work these rows only once as you work each quadrant of the design

X	DMC	A/B	Color	X	DMC	A/B	Color
3	972	298	Canary-DK	*	3716	25	Dusty Rose-VY LT
·	White	2	White	◆	3346	267	Hunter Green
−	963	73	Dusty Rose-UL VY LT	n	832	907	Golden Olive
—	310	403	Black	U	3348	264	Yellow Green-LT

"Friendship is always a sweet responsibility, never an opportunity."
~ Kahil Gibran

Pua Kenikeni XS Chart

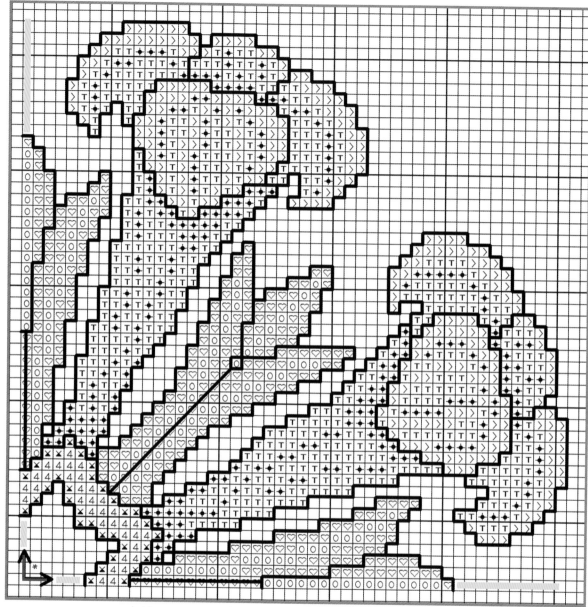

STITCH COUNT:

Total: 85 x 85
1/4 chart: 42.5 x 42.5
Center horizontal and
vertical lines share a
center stitch, as
shown by arrows

✱ When rotating
this chart, work
center rows (shown
by black arrows)
only once.

FINISHED SIZES
(approximate):

18 count: 4.75" x 4.75"
14 count: 6" x 6"
11 count: 8.5" x 8.5"

TO BACK STITCH
IN COLOR

Flowers:
Topaz DK
DMC 782
A/B 307

Leaves:
Forest Green DK
DMC 986
A/B 246

Center:
Grape DK
DMC 3834
A/B 100

work these rows only once as you work each quadrant of the design

X	DMC	A/B	Color	X	DMC	A/B	Color
T	3820	306	Straw-DK	♡	989	242	Forest Green
>	3822	295	Straw-LT	o	986	246	Forest Green-VY DK
✦	782	308	Topaz-DK	4	3836	1017	Grape-LT
—	310	403	Black	✕	3834	100	Grape-DK

"Make new friends and keep the old, one is silver and the other gold"
~ Girl Scouts Motto

128

Spiderlily
XS Chart

STITCH COUNT:

Total: 91 x 91
1/4 chart: 45.5 x 45.5
Center horizontal and
vertical lines share a
center stitch, as
shown by arrows

✱ When rotating
this chart, work
center rows (shown
by black arrows)
only once.

FINISHED SIZES
(approximate):

18 count: 5" x 5"
14 count: 6.5" x 6.5"
11 count: 8.5" x 8.5"

TO BACK STITCH
IN COLOR

Flowers:
Mauve DK
DMC 3803
A/B 972

Leaves:
Hunter Green VY DK
DMC 895
A/B 1044

Center:
Navy Blue Medium
DMC 311
A/B 148

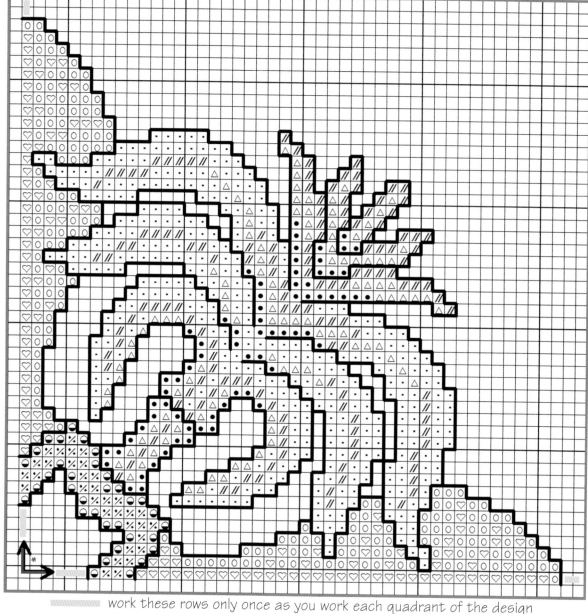

work these rows only once as you work each quadrant of the design

X	DMC	A/B	Color		X	DMC	A/B	Color
·	White	2	White		♡	989	242	Forest Green
∕∕	3689	49	Mauve-LT		○	986	246	Forest Green-VY DK
△	368	66	Mauve-MD		%	3766	167	Peacock Blue-LT
•	3803	972	Mauve-MD		◑	3765	170	Peacock Blue-VY DK
—	310	403	Black					

"We will be friends until forever, just you wait and see."
~ Winnie the Pooh

130

Star
Flower
XS Chart

STITCH COUNT:

Total: 111 x 111
1/4 chart: 55.5 x 55.5
Center horizontal and
vertical lines share a
center stitch, as
shown by arrows

* When rotating
this chart, work
center rows (shown
by black arrows)
only once.

FINISHED SIZES
(approximate):

18 count: 6.25" x 6.25"
14 count: 8" x 8"
11 count: 10" x 10"

TO BACK STITCH
IN COLOR

Flowers:
Shell Gray DK
DMC 451
A/B 233

Leaves:
Medium Avocado
Green
DMC 937
A/B 268

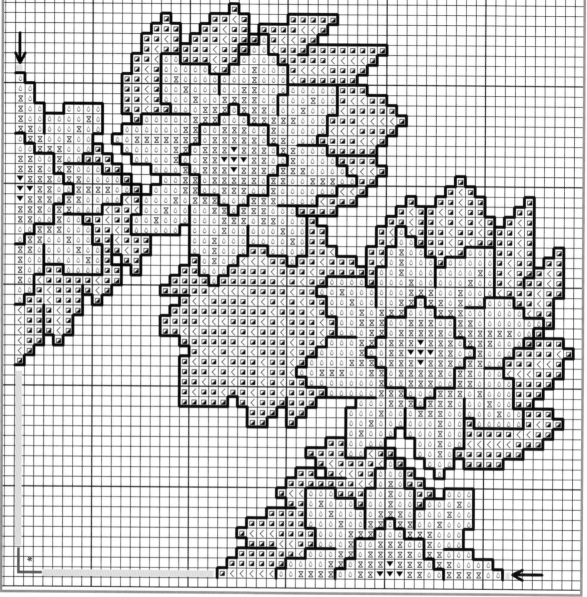

work these rows only once as you work each quadrant of the design

X	DMC	A/B	Color	X	DMC	A/B	Color
<	166	279	Moss Green-MD LT	◊	3865	2	Winter White
◪	581	280	Moss Green	⊠	Ecru	387	Ecru
▼	3013	842	Khaki Green-LT	—	310	403	Black

*"If I had a star for everytime you made me smile,
I'd have a whole night's sky in the palm of my hands."* ~ Unknown

Tahitian Gardenia XS Chart

STITCH COUNT:

Total: 115 x 115
1/4 chart: 57.5 x 57.5
Center horizontal and
vertical lines share a
center stitch, as
shown by arrows

* When rotating
this chart, work
center rows (shown
by black arrows)
only once.

FINISHED SIZES
(approximate):

18 count: 6.5" x 6.5"
14 count: 8.25" x 8.25"
11 count: 10.5" x 10.5"

TO BACK STITCH
IN COLOR

Flowers:
Steel Gray DK
DMC 414
A/B 235

Leaves:
Avocado Green VY DK
DMC 936
A/B 269

Center:
Mahogany VY DK
DMC 300
A/B 352

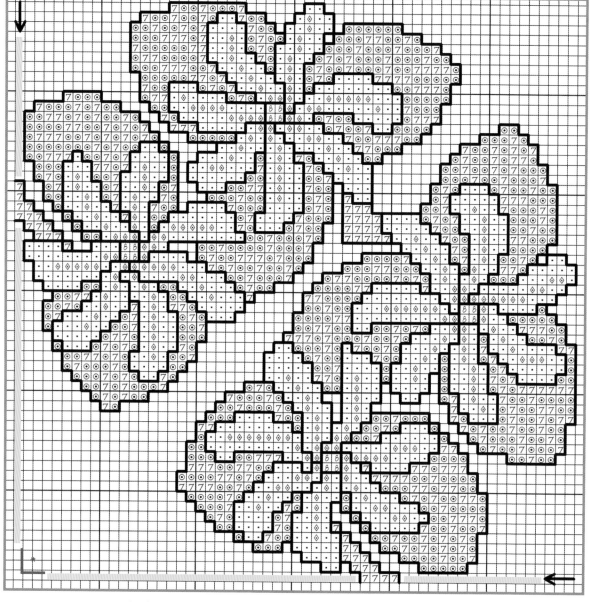

work these rows only once as you work each quadrant of the design

X	DMC	A/B	Color	X	DMC	A/B	Color
·	White	2	White	7	471	266	Avocado Green-VY LT
⑧	301	1049	Mahogany-MD	⊙	469	267	Avocado Green
◇	762	234	Pearl Gray-VY LT	—	310	403	Black

"I get by with a little help from my friends."
~ John Lennon and Paul McCartney

Torch Ginger XS Chart

STITCH COUNT:

Total: 93 x 93
1/4 chart: 46.5 x 46.5
Center horizontal and vertical lines share a center stitch, as shown by arrows

✳ When rotating this chart, work center rows (shown by black arrows) only once.

FINISHED SIZES (approximate):

18 count: 5.25" x 5.25"
14 count: 6.75" x 6.75"
11 count: 8.5" x 8.5"

TO BACK STITCH IN COLOR

Flowers:
Carnation DK
DMC 891
A/B 35

Leaves:
Hunter Green VY DK
DMC 895
A/B 268

Center:
Topaz DK
DMC 982
A/B 307

work these rows only once as you work each quadrant of the design

X	DMC	A/B	Color	X	DMC	A/B	Color
⊿	726	295	Topaz-LT	▫	893	28	Carnation-LT
−	963	73	Dusty Rose-UL VY LT	U	3348	264	Yellow Green-LT
e	894	27	Carnation-VY LT	◆	3346	267	Hunter Green-
—	310	403	Black	3	972	298	Canary-DK

"My best friend is the one who brings out the best in me."
~ Henry Ford

Vinca
XS Chart

STITCH COUNT:

Total: 113 x 113
1/4 chart: 56.5 x 56.5
Center horizontal and
vertical lines share a
center stitch, as
shown by arrows

* When rotating
this chart, work
center rows (shown
by black arrows)
only once.

FINISHED SIZES
(approximate):

18 count: 6.5" x 6.5"
14 count: 8.25" x 8.25"
11 count: 10.5" x 10.5"

TO BACK STITCH
IN COLOR

Flowers:
Blue Violet VY DK
DMC 333
A/B 119

Leaves:
Hunter Green VY DK
DMC 895
A/B 1044

Small Branches:
Golden Olive DK
DMC 830
A/B 277

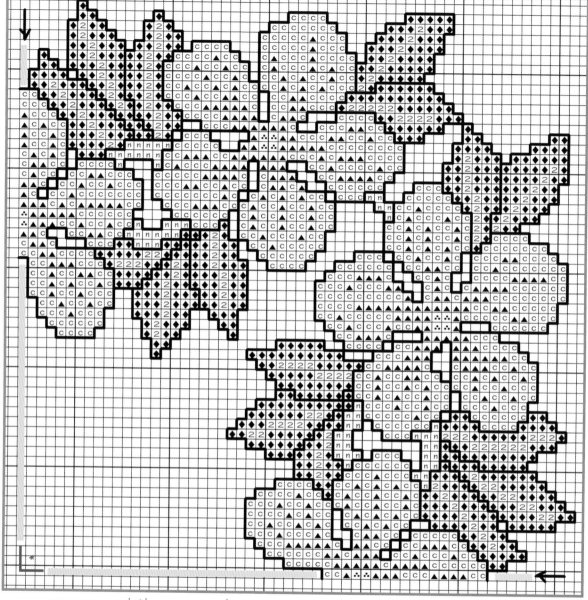

work these rows only once as you work each quadrant of the design

X	DMC	A/B	Color	X	DMC	A/B	Color
2	772	259	Yellow Green-VY LT	c	155	109	Blue Violet-MD DK
◆	3346	267	Hunter Green	▲	333	119	Blue Violet-VY DK
⋰	445	288	Lemon-LT	n	832	907	Golden Olive
—	310	403	Black				

"It is one of the blessings of old friends that you can afford to be stupid with them."
~ Ralph Waldo Emerson

Using the charts in this book

All the charts in this book use full cross stitches, so the charts may also be easily used for counted needlepoint. The nice thing about charting Hawaiian Quilt designs is that you only have to chart one-quarter of the design. The stitcher can then simply turn the chart 90 degrees when finished with one section and continue turning the chart until the design is finished.

All of the designs have an odd stitch count vertically and horizontally. Therefore, the center straight rows on the chart (marked in yellow on the diagram below) are only worked <u>once</u>. When the first section has been completely stitched and the chart is turned 90 degrees to begin another quarter section, the stitcher should start at the second row of symbols on the chart.

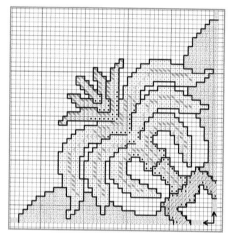

Work these center rows only once as you work each quadrant of the design.

Determining the Size of Your Finished Design

Each design has a finished size chart based on 11 and 14 count fabrics. If you are using a different count than those shown, divide the total number of stitches vertically, and then horizontally, by the count of your fabric to find the finished design size. For example: a stitch count of 110 x 110 worked on 11 count Aida would be a 10" x 10" design area; worked on 14 count fabric, the size would be just under 8" x 8".

Fabric

You may use any even weave fabric; if using linen, you would work over two threads. There is a wealth of fabrics that can be used for counted cross stitch including Aida (most commonly used), Hardanger, Lugana, etc.

Needles

Needles should be the blunt tapestry type that slip through the fabric without piercing it. Your local needlework shop can help you find the correct needle size to use. A good rule of thumb is to use a #24 needle for 11 and 14 count fabrics and a #26 needle for 16 to 22 count fabrics.

Embroidery floss

Codes for both Anchor/Bates and DMC are included. A good working length is 18 inches. The finished look will be smoother if you separate the strands of the thread and then recombine the number you wish to use. The chart will indicate how many strands were used to stitch the sample. You can certainly use more of less strands – whatever you are comfortable stitching with. Floss that twists while you work may be straightened by dangling your threaded needle and letting it spin out the twist.

Scissors

There are several brands of scissors made especially for working with counted cross stitch. They are basically medical surgical suture scissors that are slightly blunt and have a little half-moon cutout in the bottom blade. Carefully slip the stitched thread you want to cut into the cutout and then cut it without also cutting into your fabric.

Hoop or Frame

Using a hoop or frame will make for a more perfect stitching environment as it will keep your fabric taut and the weave of the fabric in place and make your stitches more consistent. Either should be large enough to surround the finished working area so that you don't have to reposition it during stitching. If using a hoop, avoid your threads catching on the clamp (or screw) while stitching by positioning it position it at 11 o'clock if you're right-handed and at 1 o'clock if you're left-handed.

Cutting the fabric

Cut the fabric about 2 to 3 inches larger than the size of the design area or large enough to conform with your intended style of finishing. Allow for seam or turning allowance if you will be framing or making your masterpiece into a pillow or other sewn project.

Centering the design

Center by folding your fabric into quarters. Mark the centerpoint with a blue pen mark at the NSEW edges or make a cross with a black basting thread. This point corresponds with the point where the vertical and horizontal arrows intersect on the graph. All of the charts in this book have an odd number stitch count. You will work the first quarter of the design exactly as shown on the chart. Working in a clockwise direction, you will start with the second row of stitching.

Reading the graph

Always make a working copy of your chart that you can mark on as you stitch. You can enlarge it to read it more easily. Mark off the completed stitches with a colored pen or highlighter as you have completed an area of them. If desired, you can also baste a grid that corresponds with the grid on your chart, taking the basting stitch out as you get to a new area. On these charts it might be a good idea to at least baste the center four squares as you will be dropping a line of stitching, starting with the second quarter.

To Begin Stitching

Do not knot the end of your thread. Bring your threaded needle up through the fabric, leaving a one inch "tail" on the reverse side. As you stitch, secure the "tail" with the stitches being made on the reverse side.

Continuing a Color in a New Area

To continue from one same color area to another, you may run your thread through stitches on the back of the work until you reach the new stitching area. It is best to end and then again begin your thread (especially dark colors) if you are traveling your thread more than an inch to a new area.

Ending Your Thread

To end, travel about an inch of your thread through previously worked stitches on the back, take a backstitch and clip the thread. Do not knot your thread. If you are "traveling" a thread on the reverse side of the work, do not travel two threads behind the same row of stitches. Doing so may cause the stitches on the front to be pulled tighter than the rest, ruining a smooth look to your completed work. Neatness counts on both sides. Remember, other stitchers looking at your masterpiece will also look at the back of your work.

Cleaning Your Work

No matter how careful you've tried to be while stitching – it's usually necessary. First, make sure that the fabric and embroidery are color safe. Soak it in cold water briefly. Use a mild detergent if necessary. Do not wring out the fabric. Rather, put it on a towel and roll it to remove excess water. Lay it on a clean dry towel, right side down. Using a colorfast cloth and a warm iron, iron until dry.

Finishing Your Work

You can frame your needlework yourself or have it done professionally. Or you can make the completed work into a pillow or insert it into myriad items that have been specially made for finished needlework. Be sure to plan your method of finishing before cutting your fabric so that if special dimensions are needed you will have sufficient fabric to meet them.

Stitching Methods

The Poke and Pull method is when the needle is pushed through the fabric from one side and pulled snug from the other. This method takes longer, but gives a very smooth look to the finished stitching. The Sewing method allows you to do the majority of your stitching from the top of the fabric. It is usually faster but the stitches are raised rather than lying flat and not always consistent.

The Cross-stitch

All of the designs in this book use full cross stitches. Bring threaded needle up at 1, down at 2, up at 3 and down at 4 (Diagram A).

Adjoining stitches of the same color may be worked in rows until the color area is completed. Rows are usually worked, starting from left to right, from top of fabric in rows to bottom. First, a half cross-stitch is made for each stitch (square) for the length of the row to be worked. Then the other half of the stitch is made in the opposite direction until the return row is completed (Diagram B).

All of the top stitches should lie in the same direction when finished. As with quilting, your mood will be reflected in your stitching. Work when you are calm and peaceful.

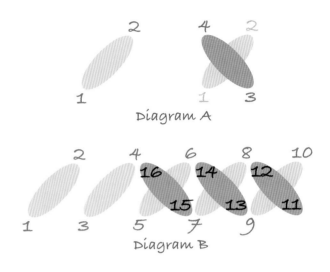

Diagram A

Diagram B

The Back Stitch

This stitch is used to outline the edge of the stitched design area or to identify areas or specific areas within the worked design. It is done after all the counted cross-stitch has been completed. Suggested colors for backstitching different areas have been included for each of the designs in this book. Black, unless indicated, is often too harsh for a design. Deciding what color to use is a matter of personal taste.

Use one ply of the six-ply embroidery floss for backstitching. For designs that need a bolder outline, use one less strand than was used to stitch the design.

To backstitch, bring the threaded needle up at 1, down at 2, up at 3, down at 2, up at 4, down at 3, etc. (Diagram C). Take care not to snag threads already worked.

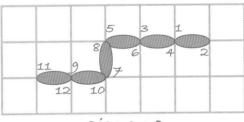

Diagram C

"A single rose can be my garden...
a single friend, my world."
~Leo Buscaglia

Fabric Credits

 Many of the fabrics used in the quilts in this book are from these well-known fabric companies:

BENARTEX, INC.
Fabric: Fossil Fern

1359 Broadway, Suite 1100
New York, NY 10018
www.benartex.com

HOFFMAN CALIFORNIA FABRICS
Fabric: Batiks, Hand dyed and Solids

25792 Obrero Drive
Mission Viejo, CA 92691
www.hoffmanfabrics.com

KONA BAY FABRICS
Fabric: Kona Cotton Solids

1637 Kahai Street
Honolulu, HI 96819
www.konabay.com

MODA FABRICS / UNITED NOTIONS
Fabric: Hand dyed

13795 Hutton
Dallas, TX 75234
www.modafabrics.com

THE WARM COMPANY
Batting: Warm & White, Soft & Black

954 E Union Street
Seattle, WA 98122
www.warmcompany.com

Please visit the web sites of these popular manufacturers to find out what's new and to locate the local quilting shops in your area where you will find these fine fabrics.

About Al Hannen

 Little did Al Hannen know, during his high school years in Miles, Montana, or while attending college at UC Santa Barbara or traveling around the world during his stint in the US Air Force, that he would not only be charting and stitching his own counted cross stitch designs – but also offering them to thousands of others to enjoy.

Perhaps the intricate detail of the charting appealed to him because of his twenty years in the jewelry trade where he did custom designs for customers at the small shop where he worked in Ventura, California.

Al started designing counted cross stitch in 1980. He submitted some designs for my little *Hawaiian Designin'* magazine which led to my distributing his first designs in Hawaii and later his Pacific Collection booklets that were, by then, also distributed nationally.

Al retired in 1990 and moved to Molokai to soak in the local culture for 18 months or so. He now lives in Medford, Oregon.

I was delighted when he agreed to share his unique color sense to chart some of my Hawaiian quilt designs in this book. As you will see, they are true works of art.

"If you judge people, you have no time to love them."
~ Mother Teresa

 For many, in what should be their golden years, life is not easy. Fine individuals who paved the way over past decades for their families and many times, directly or indirectly, for ours.

Those on fixed incomes, those with debilitating medical costs, those without family to help, those confused and unable to cope with the daily living decisions and activities we all take for granted each day. It is our responsibility as well as our honor to make the last years of their lives comfortable – to care for them as they once cared for us...our family, now elderly, who may have given us our first glimpse at and continuing appreciation of a handmade quilt.

To help, in small part, a portion of the proceeds of *Friendship Quilts...the Hawaiian Way* will be donated to the Catholic Charities Hawaii Elderly Services which are available to all eligible persons regardless of race, color, creed, religion, national origin, sex, marital status, sexual orientation, public assistance status, disability or age.

Their multifaceted program makes it possible for senior citizens of all faiths to continue living full and independent lives in the community. The agency works to help delay or prevent institutionalization of the elderly by providing supportive services, as well as advocates for social justice on their behalf.

They serve elders with compassion and empower them to maintain their independence and dignity, including chore/housekeeping, transportation, housing assistance, respite linkages, money management, adult foster home placement, case management, and senior center activities at the Lanakila Multi-Purpose Senior Center.

You can learn more about their services
on their comprehensive website at:
www.CatholicCharitiesHawaii.org.
Volunteers and donations are always welcome.

 CATHOLIC CHARITIES HAWAI'I

Elizabeth's Hawaiian Quilt Bookshelf

If we've piqued your curiosity about Hawaiian Quilting, look for these other Elizabeth Root books.

"Menehune Quilts... the Hawaiian Way"

Twenty miniature size (24"x 24") patterns for single and multi-color projects. Fully illustrated Hawaiian quilt history and quilting instructions.

"Honor Each Quilt"

A hardcover journal for quilters or quilt collectors to showcase 95 separate projects. Well organized, beautifully illustrated - makes a wonderful gift.

"The Pillows to Patch Quilt Collection... the Hawaiian Way"

Thirty two pillow size (18"x18") projects including single and multicolor patterns. Also, 32 matching mini patterns.

"The Hawaiian Quilt Art Guest Book"

A pretty, unisex guest book with room for about 500 entries. Perfect for any business that collects customer information; family gatherings or special events.

"Quilting Days... the Hawaiian Way"

A practical, undated day planner with 12 months of weeks, annual calendars, addresses and phone numbers. Patterns for 15 quilt blocks with instructions.

"Cat Nap Quilts... the Hawaiian Way"

Ten 48"-72" full size patterns on two pull-out inserts. Ten matching designs for 18"-24" quilt squares. Complete illustrated instructions.

"Books and friends should be few but good."

ROOT • Menehune Quilts...the Hawaiian Way • ERDHI

ROOT THE PILLOWS TO PATCH QUILT COLLECTION...THE HAWAIIAN WAY ERDHI

ROOT QUILTING DAYS...THE HAWAIIAN WAY ERDHI

ROOT HONOR EACH QUILT My Journal of Quilts • Made and Acquired ERDHI

ROOT The Hawaiian Quilt Art Guest Book ERDHI

ROOT CAT NAP QUILTS...THE HAWAIIAN WAY ERDHI

Please visit us at www.QuiltsHawaii.com